RED HOT CHILI PEPPERS
the GETAWAY

Music transcriptions by Pete Billmann, Addi Booth and Ron Piccione

ISBN 978-1-4950-7064-8

7777 W. BLUEMOUND RD. P.O. BOX 13819 MILWAUKEE, WI 53213

In Australia Contact:
Hal Leonard Australia Pty. Ltd.
4 Lentara Court
Cheltenham, Victoria, 3192 Australia
Email: ausadmin@halleonard.com.au

Visit Hal Leonard Online at
www.halleonard.com

The Getaway

Words and Music by Anthony Kiedis, Flea, Chad Smith, Josh Klinghoffer and Brian Burton

*Bkgd. vocs.: Anna Waronker

Dark Necessities

Words and Music by Anthony Kiedis, Flea, Chad Smith, Josh Klinghoffer and Brian Burton

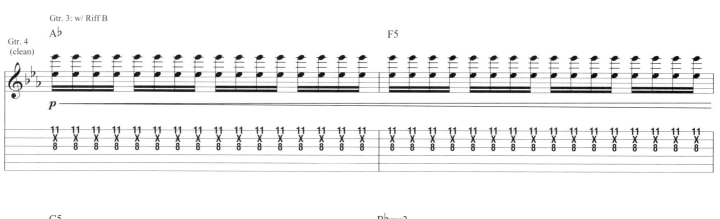

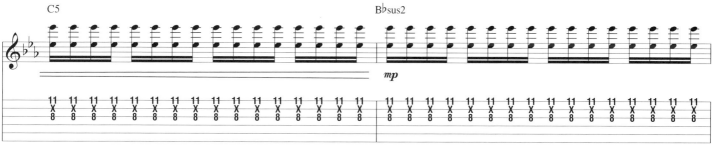

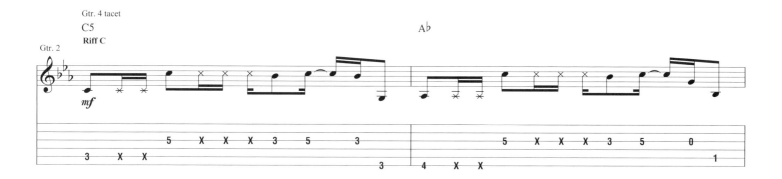

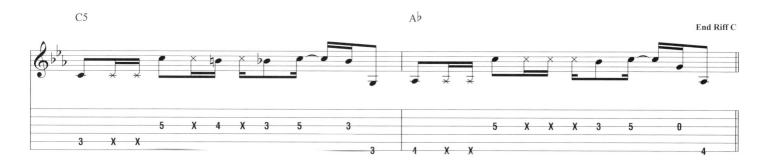

Verse

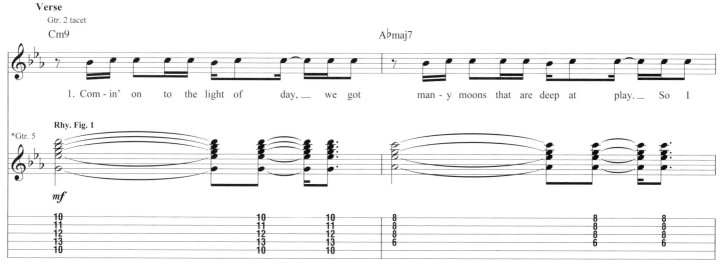

1. Com - in' on to the light of day,__ we got man - y moons that are deep at play.__ So I

*Piano arr. for gtr.

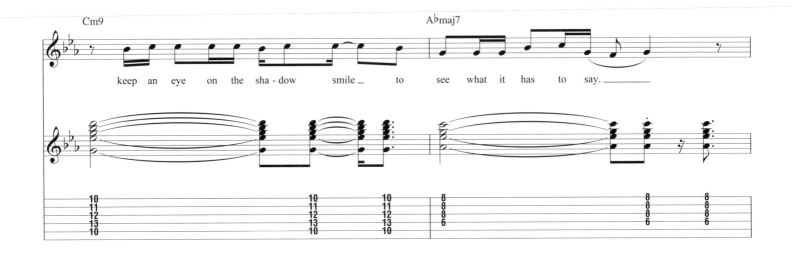

keep an eye on the sha-dow smile __ to see what it has to say. ____

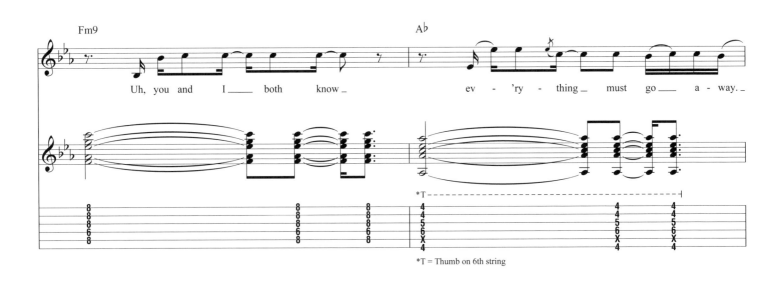

Uh, you and I __ both know __ ev - 'ry - thing __ must go __ a - way. __

*T = Thumb on 6th string

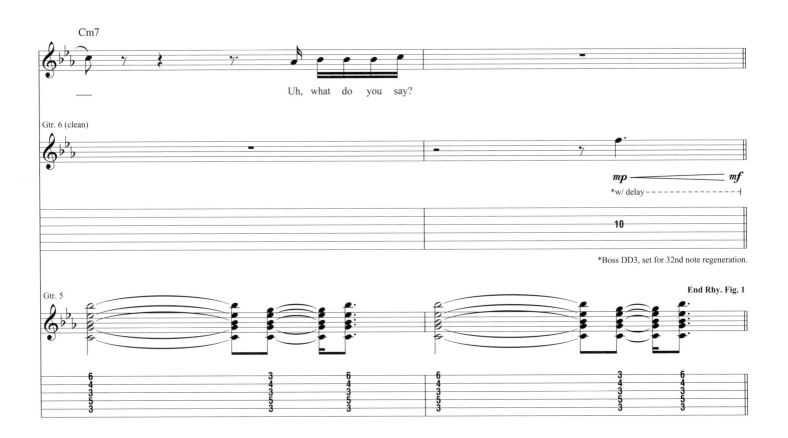

Uh, what do you say?

Gtr. 6 (clean)

mp ——— *mf*

*w/ delay- - - - - - - - - - -

*Boss DD3, set for 32nd note regeneration.

Gtr. 5

End Rhy. Fig. 1

Chorus

Uh, you don't know my mind. You don't know my kind.

Dark ne-cess-i-ties are part of my de-sign. And

(Ah,

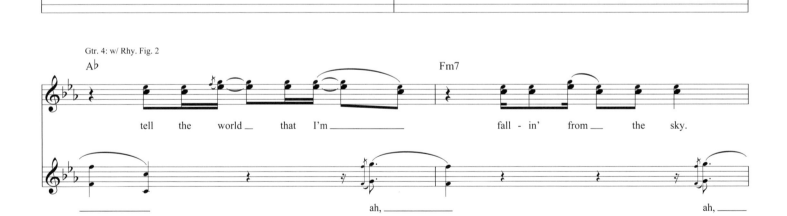

tell the world that I'm fall-in' from the sky.

ah, ah,

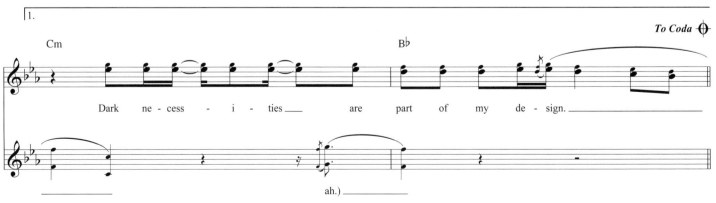

Dark ne-cess-i-ties are part of my de-sign.

ah.)

Interlude

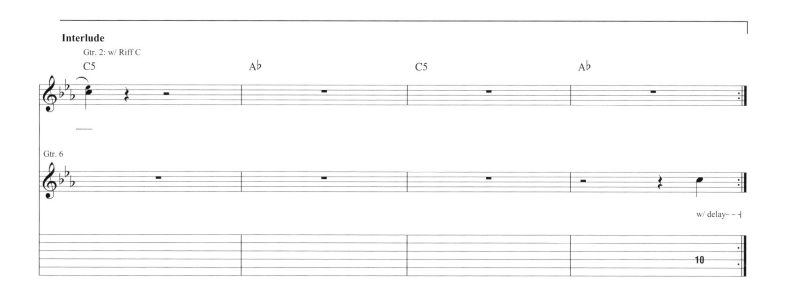

2.

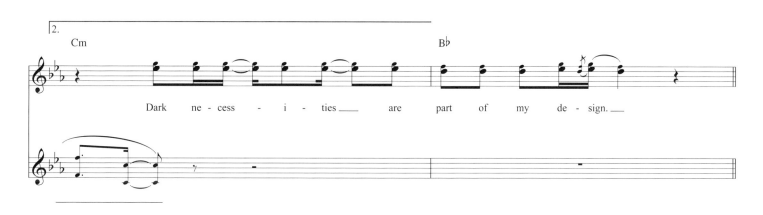

Dark ne - cess - i - ties ___ are part of my de - sign. ___

Interlude

Bridge

Do you want ___ this love ___ of mine? ___ Dark-ness helps ___ us all ___ to shine. ___ Do you want ___ it? Do you want ___ it

now? ___ Uh, do you want it all ___ the time? ___ But dark-ness helps us all ___ to shine. ___

D.S. al Coda
(take 1st ending)

Gtr. 7 tacet

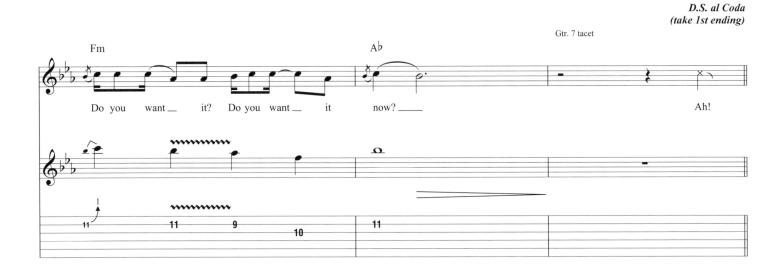

Do you want ___ it? Do you want ___ it now? ___ Ah!

Coda

Guitar Solo

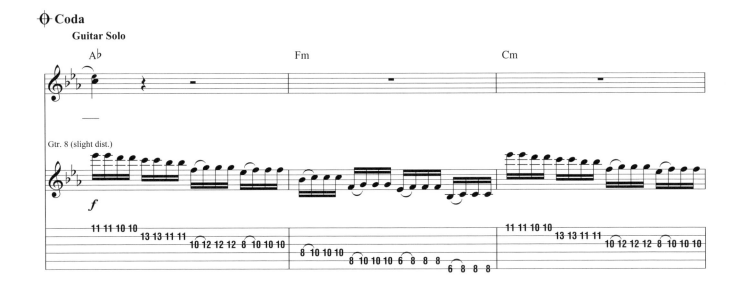

Gtr. 8 (slight dist.)

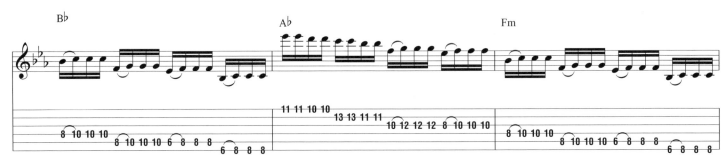

We Turn Red

Words and Music by Anthony Kiedis, Flea, Chad Smith, Josh Klinghoffer and Brian Burton

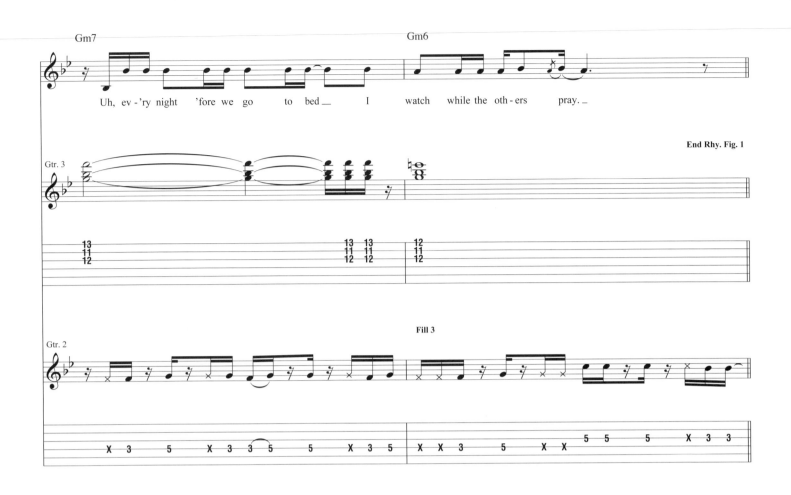

Uh, ev-'ry night 'fore we go to bed __ I watch while the oth-ers pray. __

End Rhy. Fig. 1

Fill 3

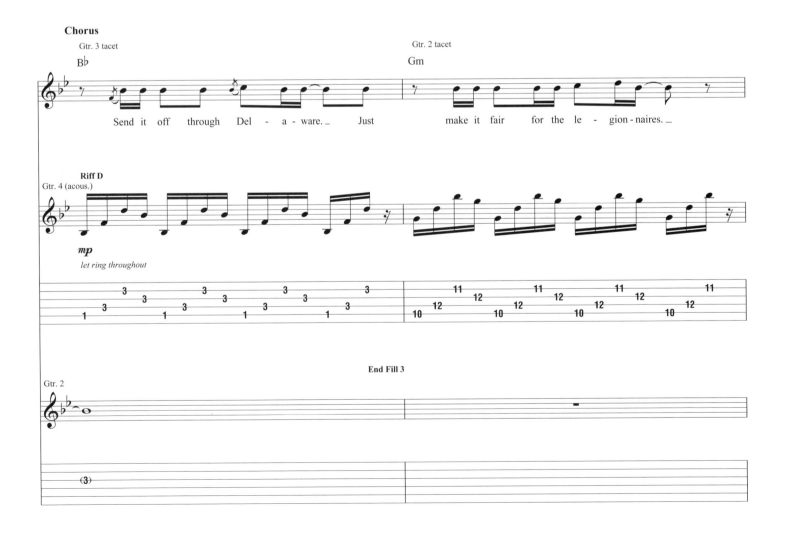

Chorus

Send it off through Del - a - ware. __ Just make it fair for the le - gion-naires. __

Riff D

mp

let ring throughout

End Fill 3

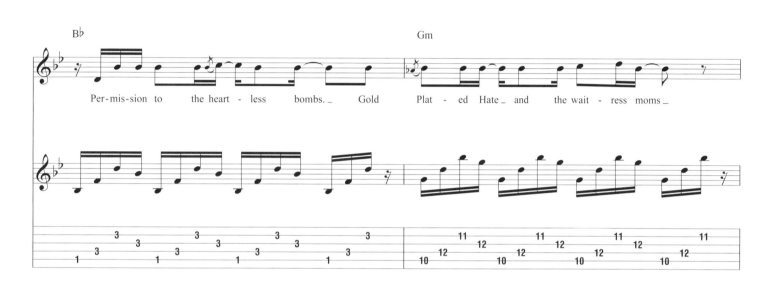

Verse

Gtr. 2: w/ Riff B
Gtr. 4 tacet

2. Mex-i-co, you are my neigh-bor. Home of the let's be brav-er.

Gtr. 5   Rhy. Fig. 2   End Rhy. Fig. 2

*w/ delay - - - - - - - - - - - - - - - -

*Set for eighth-note regeneration w/ 1 repeat.

Gtr. 2: w/ Riff C (2 times)
Gtr. 5: w/ Rhy. Fig. 2 (2 times)

Give me all your sick and your tired rac-es that we ad-mire.

Do you want to go danc-ing in Chi-ca-go? Trin-i-dad's got it bad for To-ba-go.

Gtr. 2: w/ Riff B

Take me to the lake, uh, where we do the Av-o-ca-do. Hal-le-lu-jah, a des-pe-ra-do.

Gtr. 5

w/ delay

Pre-Chorus

Gtr. 2: w/ Riff C (1 1/2 times)
Gtr. 3: w/ Rhy. Fig. 1

Sit-ting here I count the moons. The or-ders we o-beyed.

delay   w/ delay

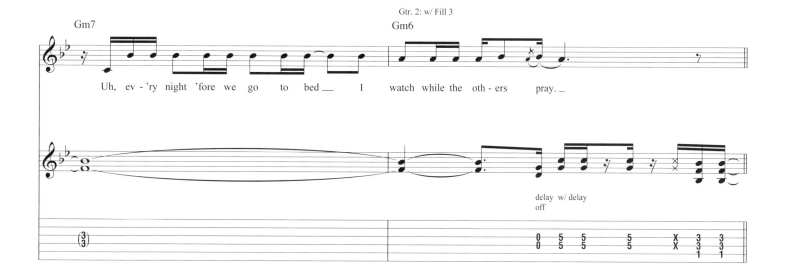

Chorus

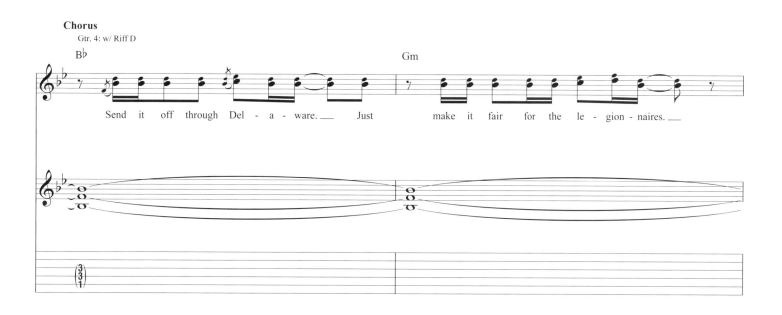

Per - mis - sion to the heart - less bombs. __ Gold Plat - ed Hate __ and the wait - ress moms __

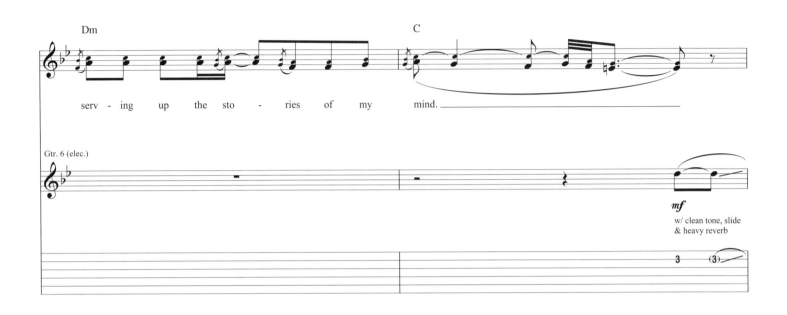

serv - ing up the sto - ries of my mind. _____

Gtr. 6 (elec.)

mf
w/ clean tone, slide
& heavy reverb

Com - ing down from the de - serts where __ you caught a glimpse of the bil - lion - aire. __

Gtr. 6

*Gtrs. 4 & 7

*Gtr. 7 (elec.) w/ clean tone & chorus, played *mf*
Composite arrangement

Tell me I'm the right ___ one for the ride. _____

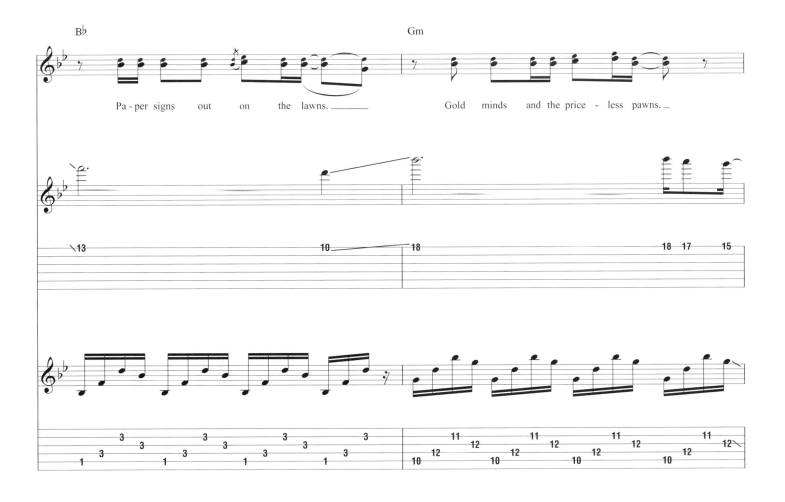

Pa - per signs out on the lawns. _____ Gold minds and the price - less pawns. __

The Longest Wave

Words and Music by Anthony Kiedis, Flea, Chad Smith and Josh Klinghoffer

Verse

seam-less lit-tle team and then we tanked. I guess we're not so sac-ro-sanct. The

tip of my tongue, but then we blanked. The wave _____ is here, _____

Interlude

wait-ing on the wind to tell _____ my side. _____

*w/ delay

*Set for dotted sixteenth-note regeneration w/ 1 repeat.

Verse

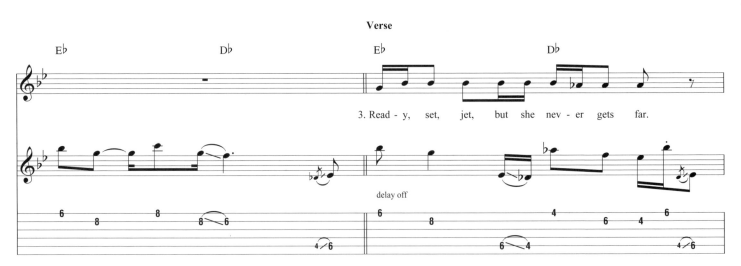

3. Read-y, set, jet, but she nev-er gets far.

delay off

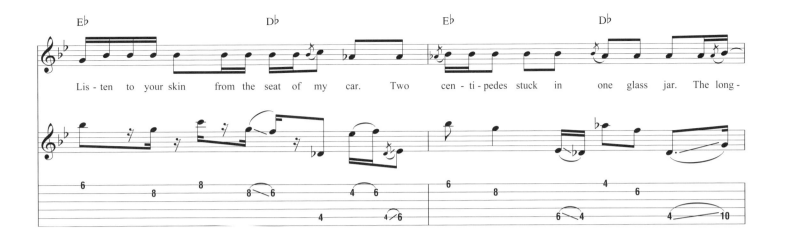

Lis - ten to your skin from the seat of my car. Two cen - ti - pedes stuck in one glass jar. The long -

- est wave, ___ wait - ing on the wind to tell ___ my side. _____

let ring - - - - - - - - - - - - - - - -

Pre-Chorus

__ What - cha want? _ What - cha need? _

Rhy. Fig. 1

w/ pick & finger

Do you love? _____

End Rhy. Fig. 1

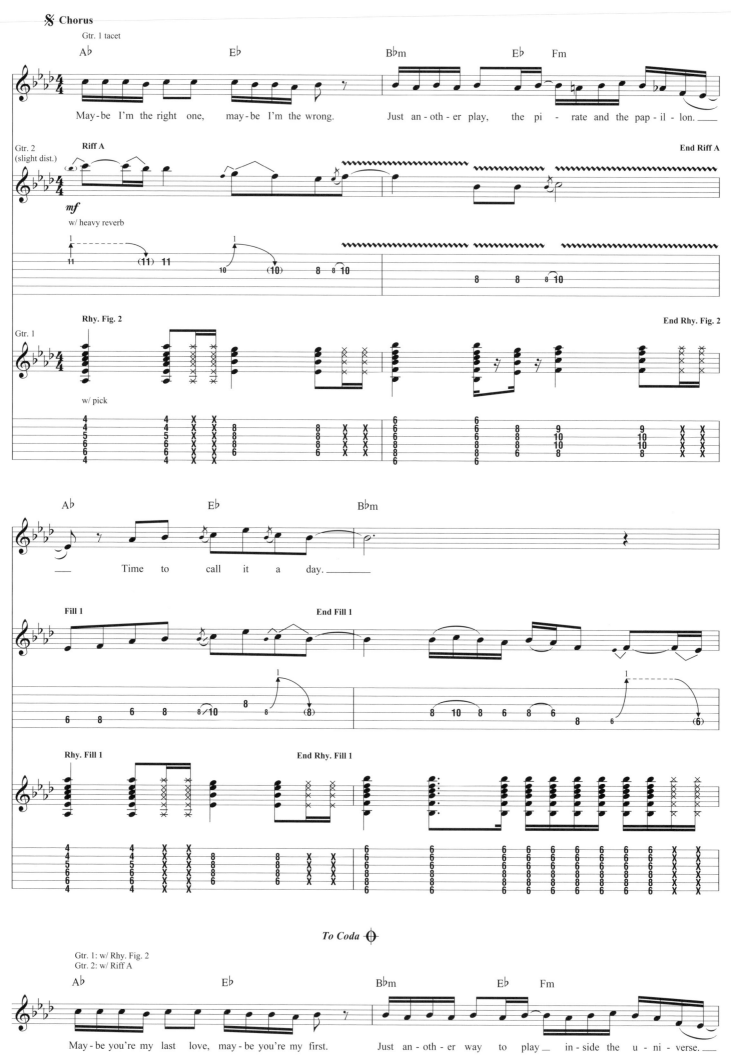

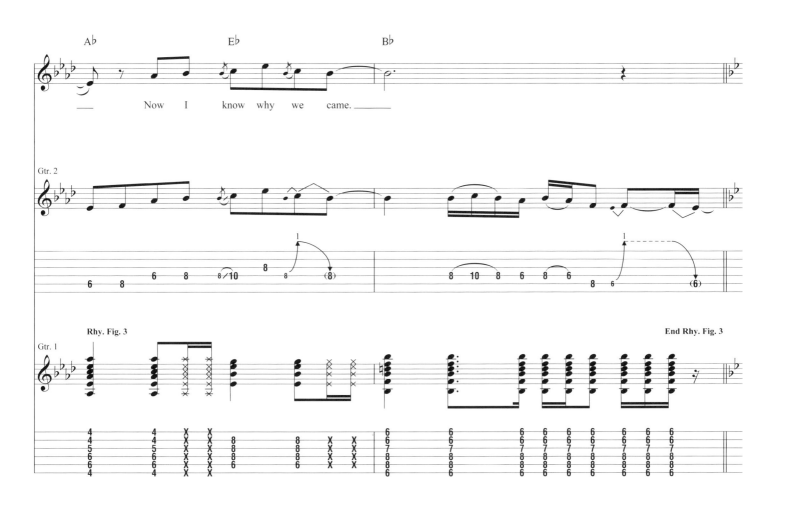

Now I know why we came.

Rhy. Fig. 3

End Rhy. Fig. 3

Verse

Gtr. 2 tacet

4. Sterile as the barrel of an old twelve gauge. Under my skin and half my age.

w/ pick & fingers

Hot - ter than the wax on a sax - i - frage. The long - est wave, __

Gtr. I

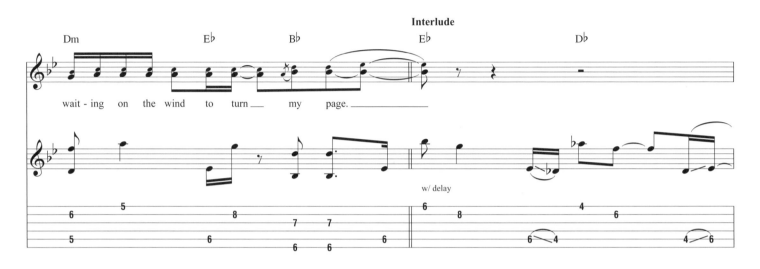

Interlude

wait - ing on the wind to turn __ my page. _____

w/ delay

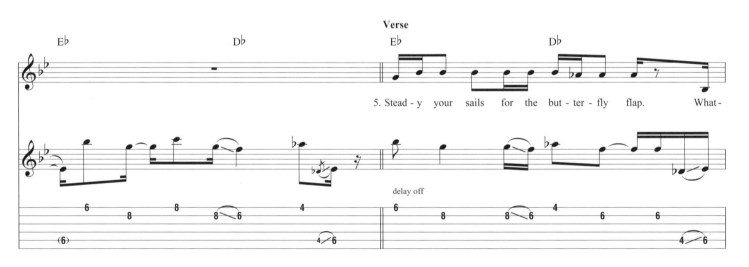

Verse

5. Stead - y your sails for the but - ter - fly flap. What -

delay off

ev - er you do, don't close that gap. I'm dream - ing of a wom - an, but she's just my nap. Your

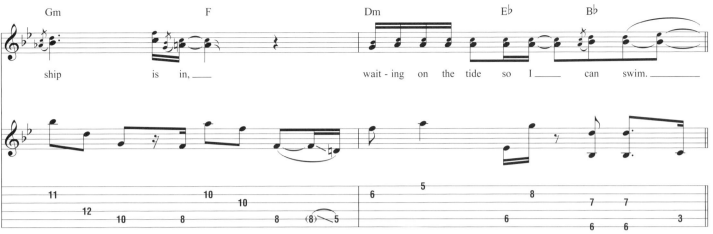

D.S. al Coda

Pre-Chorus

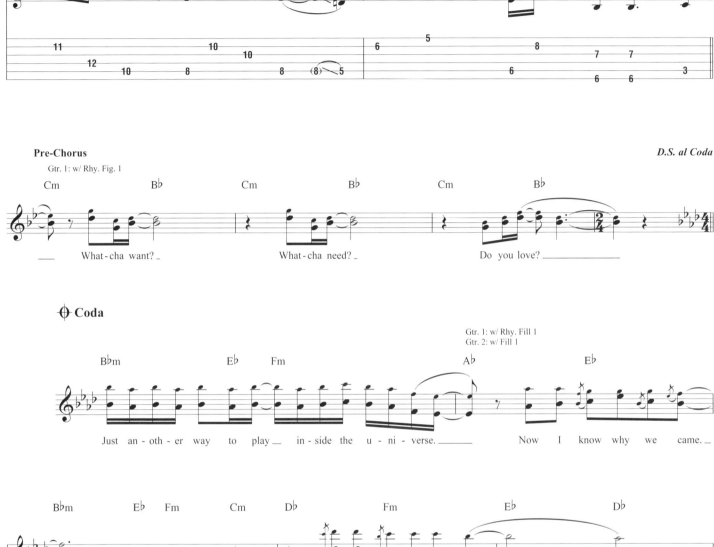

Coda

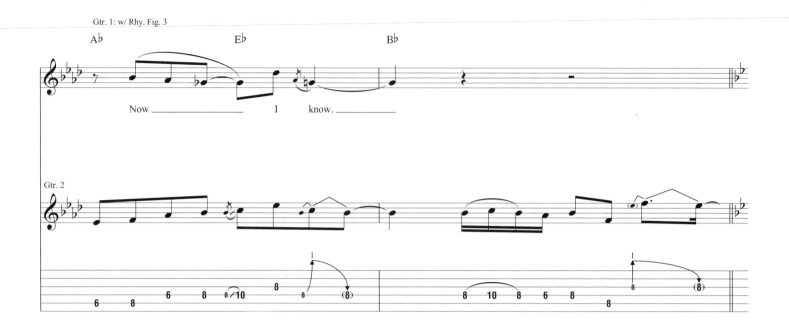

Outro

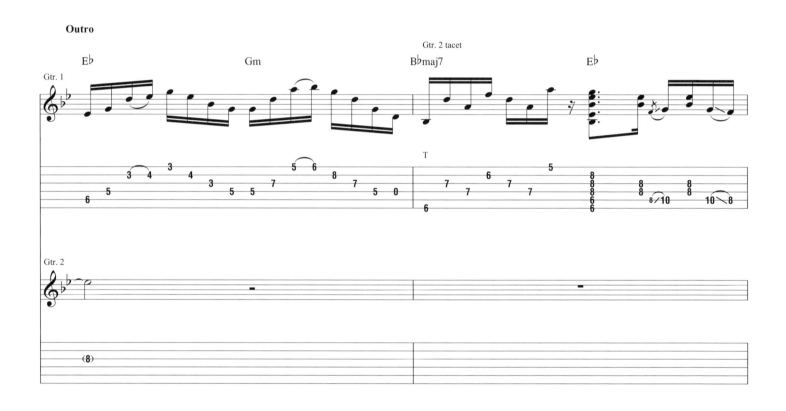

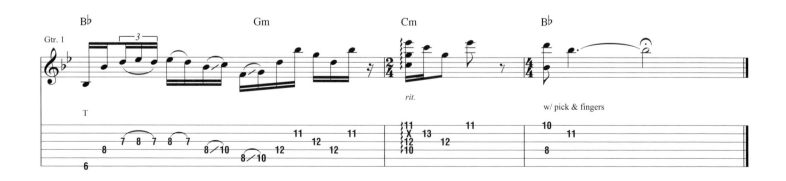

Goodbye Angels

Words and Music by Anthony Kiedis, Flea, Chad Smith and Josh Klinghoffer

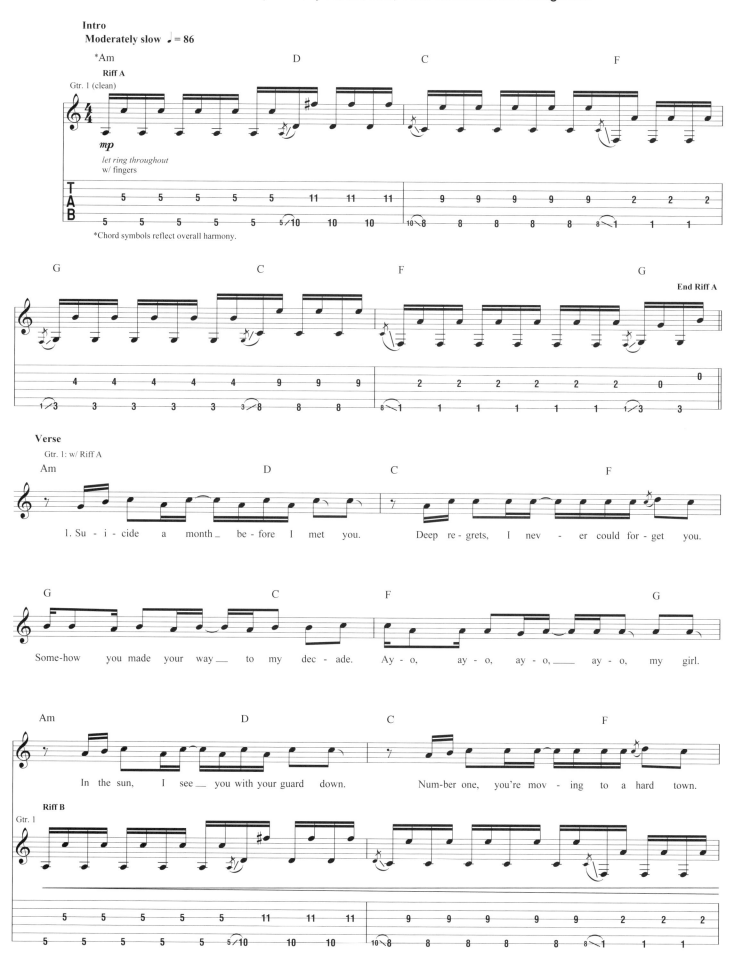

34

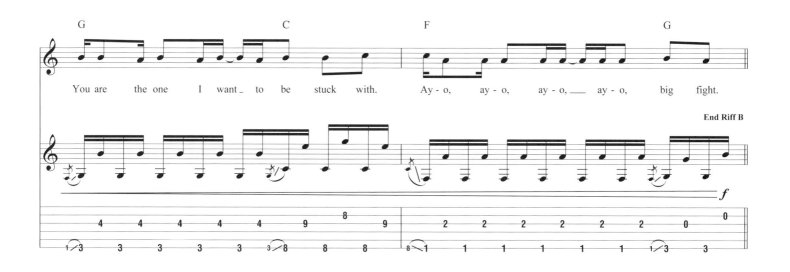

You are the one I want to be stuck with. Ay-o, ay-o, ay-o, __ ay-o, big fight.

End Riff B

Pre-Chorus

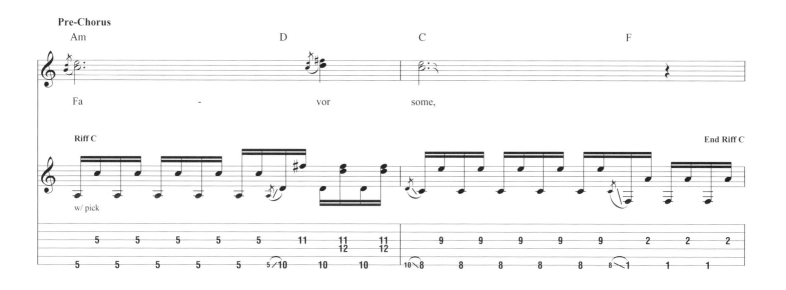

Fa - vor some,

Riff C

w/ pick

End Riff C

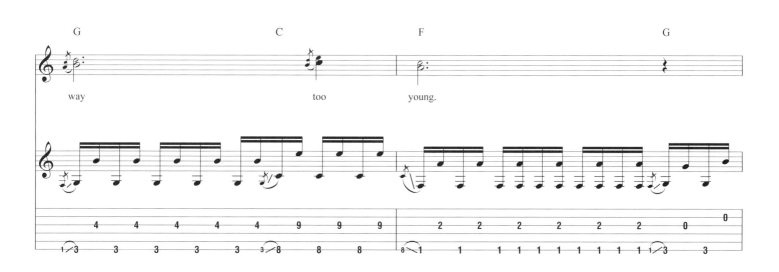

way too young.

Gtr. 1: w/ Riff C

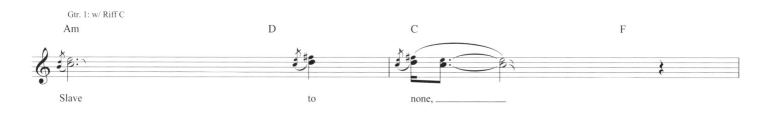

Slave to none, _____

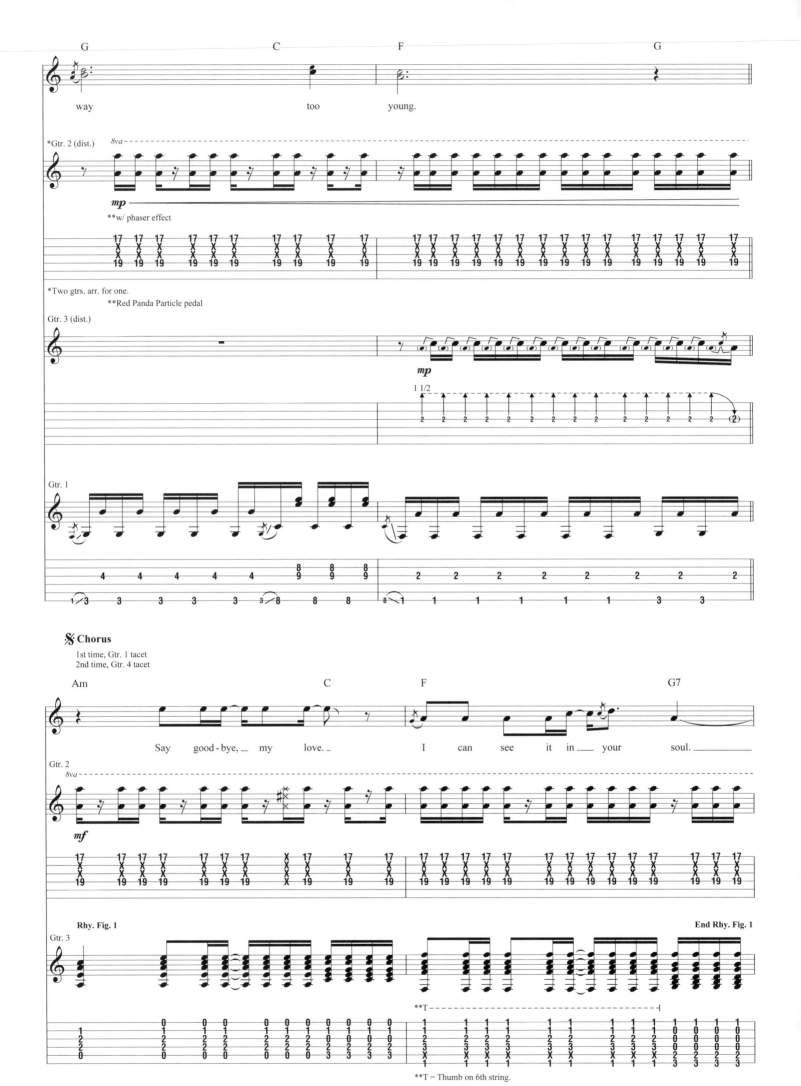

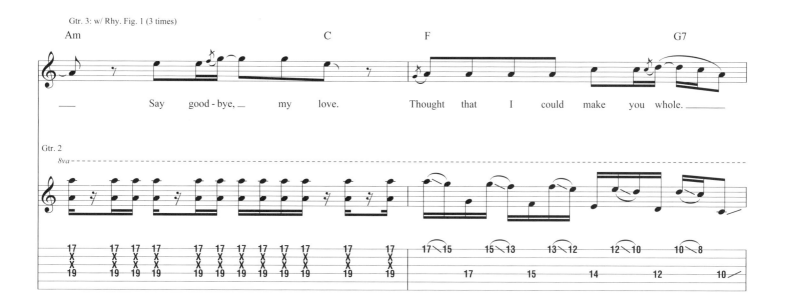

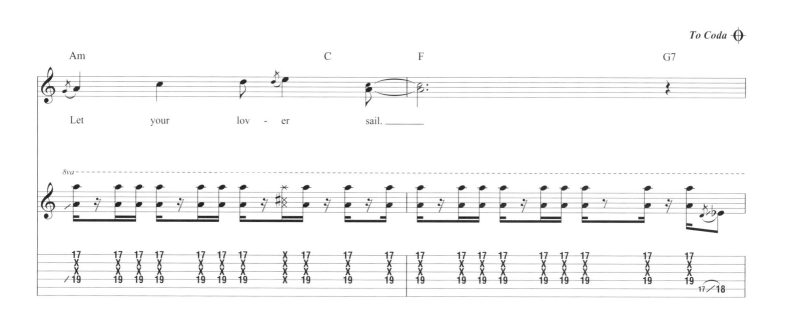

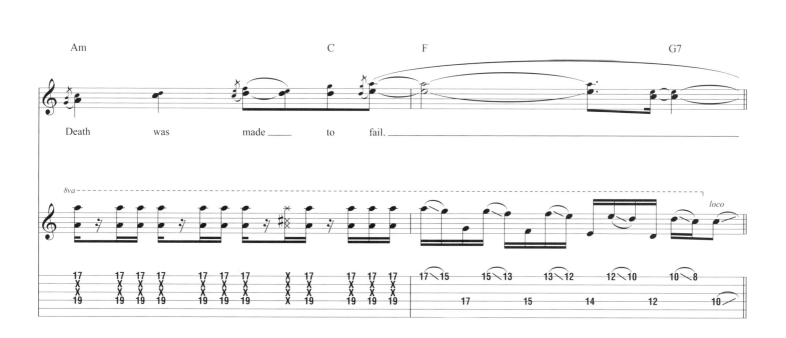

Verse

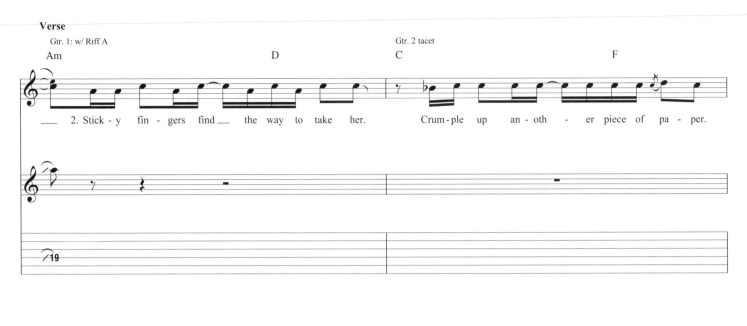

Gtr. 1: w/ Riff A
Gtr. 2 tacet

Am — D — C — F

2. Stick - y fin - gers find the way to take her. Crum - ple up an - oth - er piece of pa - per.

19

G — C — F — G

I know your days are num - bered when it comes to, ay - o, ay - o, ay - o, ay - o, this life.

Fill 1   End Fill 1

Gtr. 4 (clean)

mf
*

12   12   12 14

*w/ Red Panda Particle pedal

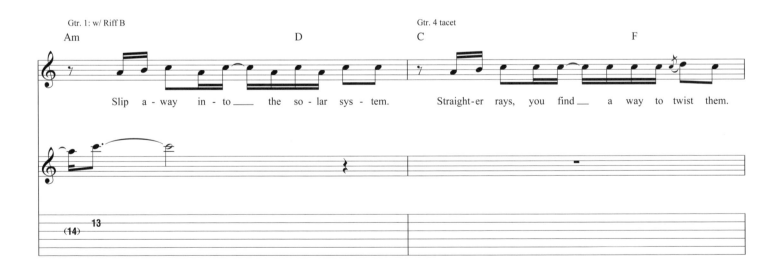

Gtr. 1: w/ Riff B
Gtr. 4 tacet

Am — D — C — F

Slip a - way in - to the so - lar sys - tem. Straight-er rays, you find a way to twist them.

(14) 13

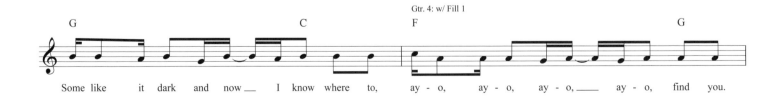

Gtr. 4: w/ Fill 1

G — C — F — G

Some like it dark and now I know where to, ay - o, ay - o, ay - o, ay - o, find you.

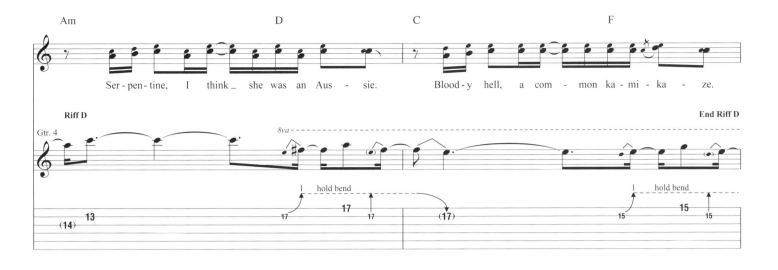

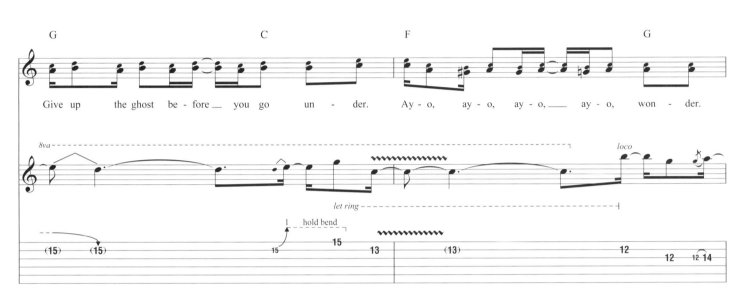

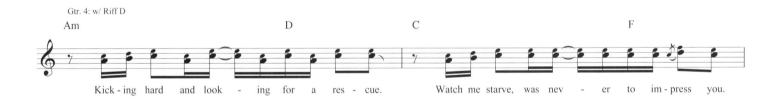

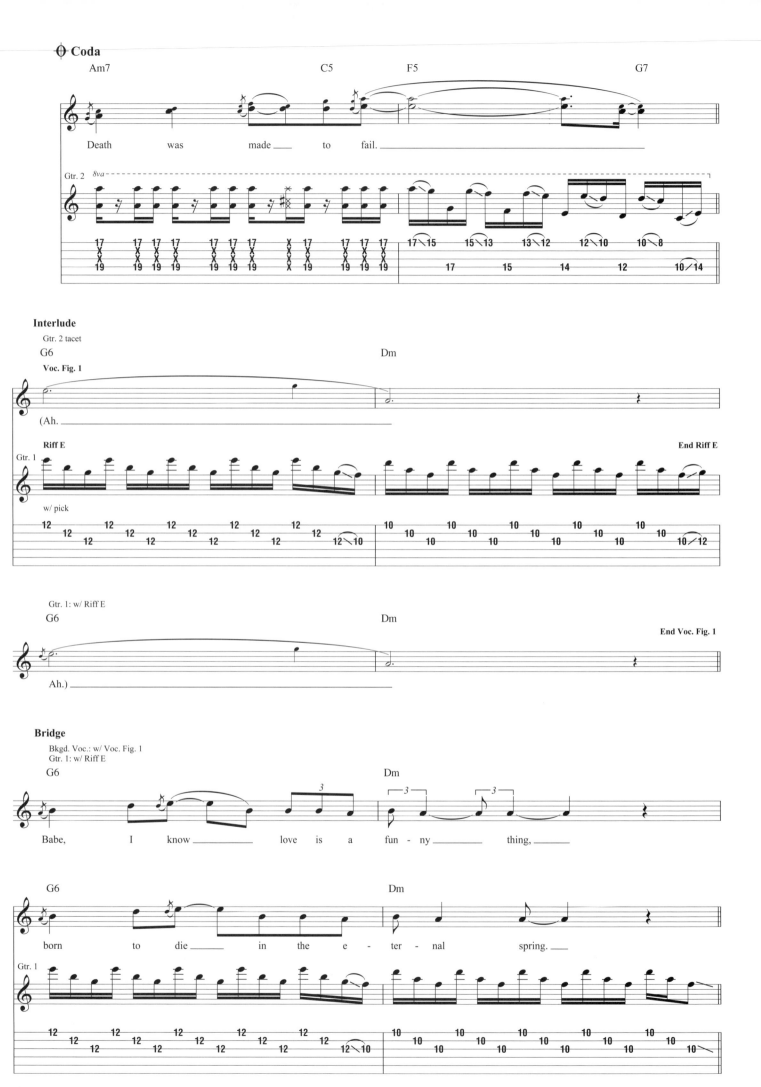

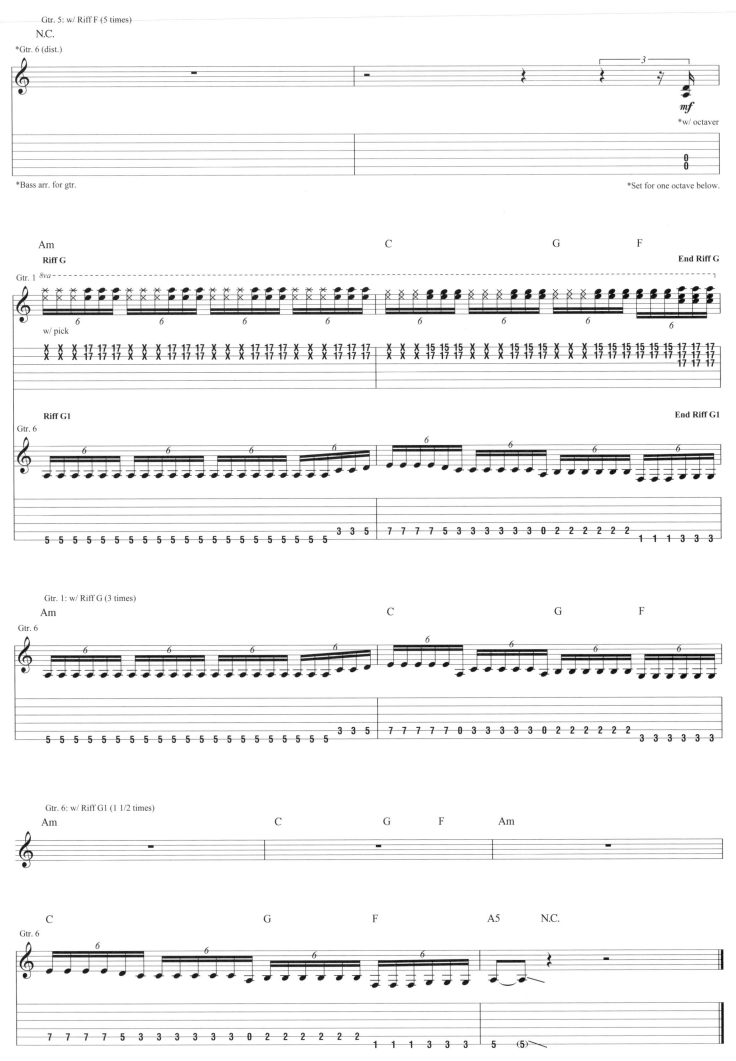

Sick Love

Words and Music by Anthony Kiedis, Flea, Chad Smith, Josh Klinghoffer, Elton John and Bernie Taupin

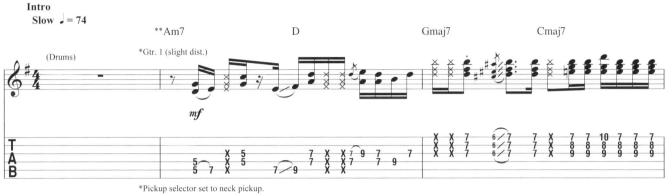

*Pickup selector set to neck pickup.
**Chord symbols reflect implied harmony.

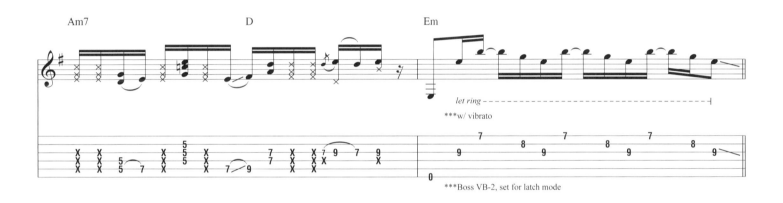

***Boss VB-2, set for latch mode

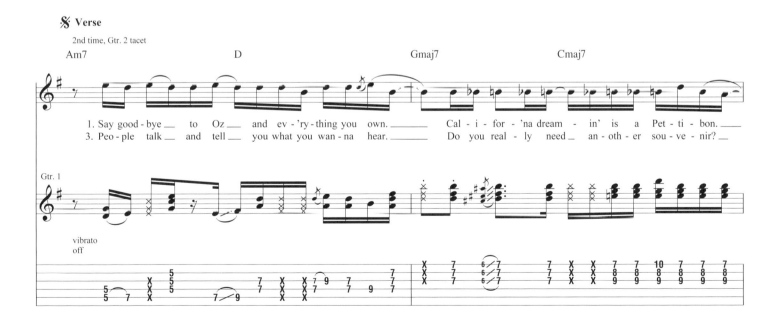

1. Say good-bye to Oz and ev-'ry-thing you own. Cal-i-for-'na dream-in' is a Pet-ti-bon.
3. Peo-ple talk and tell you what you wan-na hear. Do you real-ly need an-oth-er sou-ve-nir?

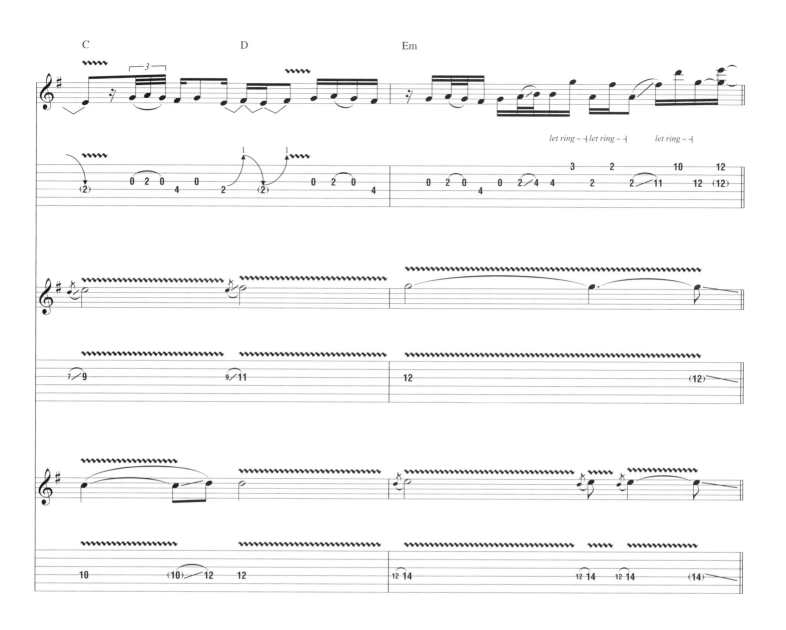

Outro-Chorus

Gtr. 2: w/ Rhy. Fig. 1 (2 times)
Gtrs. 4 & 5 tacet

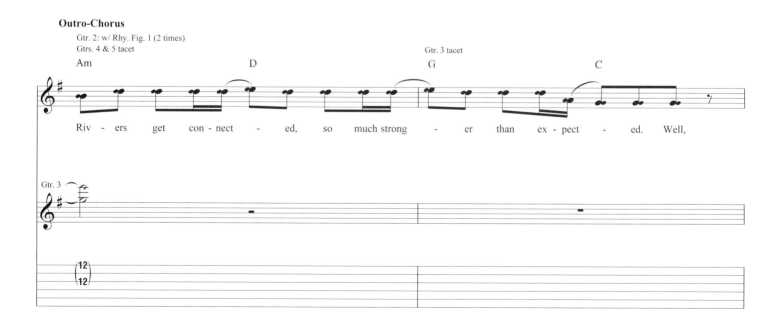

Riv - ers get con - nect - ed, so much strong - er than ex - pect - ed. Well,

sick love comes to ___ wash us a - way. ___

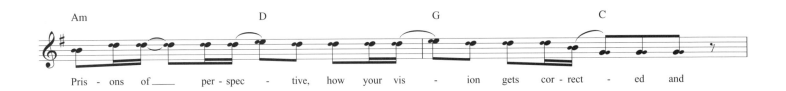

Pris - ons of ___ per - spec - tive, how your vis - ion gets cor - rect - ed and

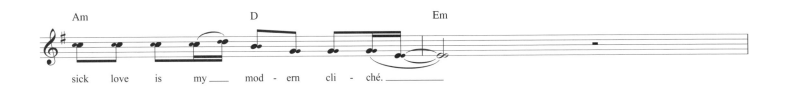

sick love is my ___ mod - ern cli - ché. ___

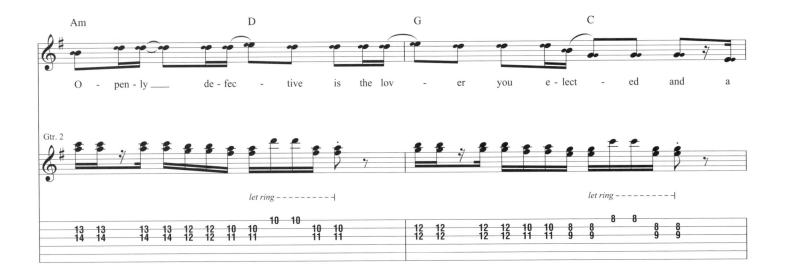

O - pen - ly ___ de - fec - tive is the lov - er you e - lect - ed and a

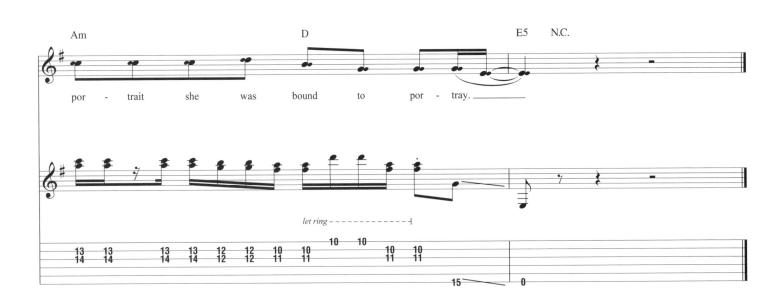

por - trait she was bound to por - tray. ___

Go Robot

Words and Music by Anthony Kiedis, Flea, Chad Smith and Josh Klinghoffer

Intro
Moderately fast ♩ = 133

*Chord symbols reflect implied harmony.

Verse

1. I called the teach-er 'cause I want-ed to con-fess it now. Can I make the time for me to come and get it blessed some-how? __ She spoke to me in such a sim-ple and de-ci-sive tone. __

Pre-Chorus

Her sweet ad-mis-sion left me feel-ing in po-si-tion from. I don't take these things __ so per-son-al __ an-y-more, __ an-y-more. __ I don't think it's ir-re-vers-i-ble __ an-y-more. __

Verse

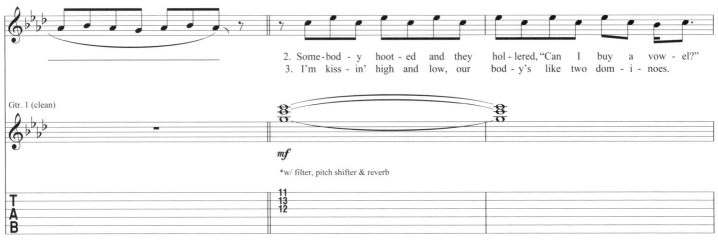

Cm

2. Some-bod - y hoot - ed and they hol - lered, "Can I buy a vow - el?"
3. I'm kiss - in' high and low, our bod - y's like two dom - i - noes.

Gtr. 1 (clean)

mf

*w/ filter, pitch shifter & reverb

*Ibanez Autofilter & Boss PS3

Fm7   Cm

Don't let her catch you in the act of throw - ing in the tow - el. And when it's not as it ap -
Can I come and get you when I hit you in your par - ty clothes? __ Let's turn this cos - play __

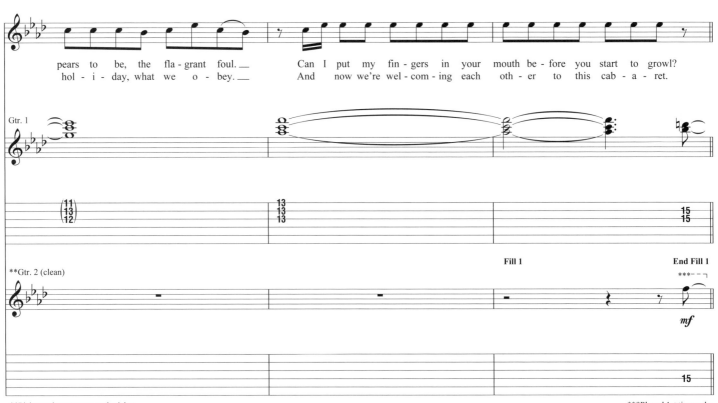

Fm7

pears to be, the fla - grant foul. __ Can I put my fin - gers in your mouth be - fore you start to growl?
hol - i - day, what we o - bey. __ And now we're wel - com - ing each oth - er to this cab - a - ret.

Gtr. 1

**Gtr. 2 (clean)

Fill 1   End Fill 1

mf

**Pickup selector set to neck pickup.   ***Played 1st time only.

Pre-Chorus

1., 3. I don't think that it's __ so ter - ri - ble __ an - y - more, __ an - y - more.
2. I don't think that it's __ so per - son - al __ an - y - more, __ an - y - more.

I don't think that it's __ un - bear - a - ble __ an - y - more. __
I don't think it's ir - re - vers - a - ble __ an - y - more. __

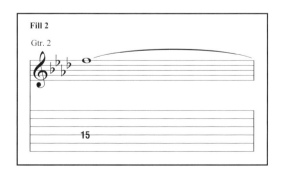

Fill 2

Gtr. 2

Feasting on the Flowers

Words and Music by Anthony Kiedis, Flea, Chad Smith, Josh Klinghoffer and Brian Burton

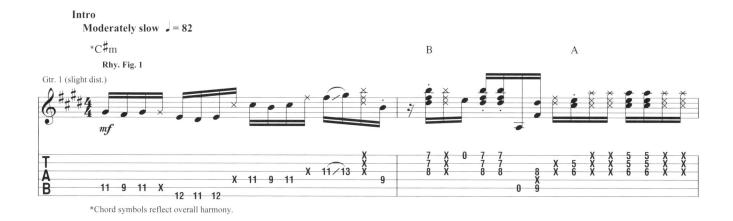

*Chord symbols reflect overall harmony.

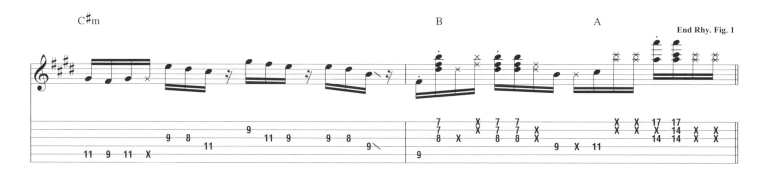

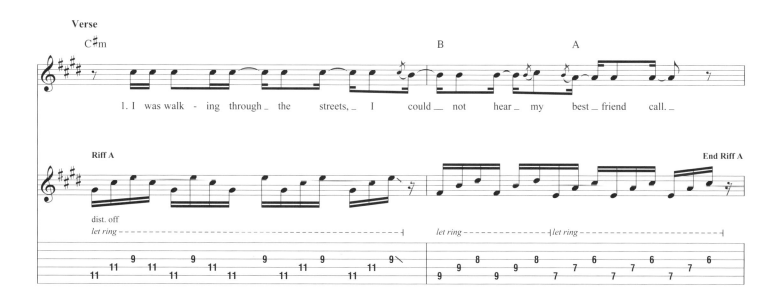

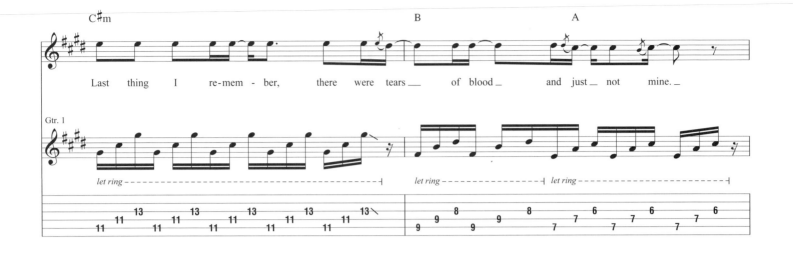

Last thing I re-mem-ber, there were tears ___ of blood ___ and just ___ not ___ mine. ___

Uh, an-y oth - er day ___ and I ___ would save ___ you from this cold ___ de - cline.

𝄉 Chorus

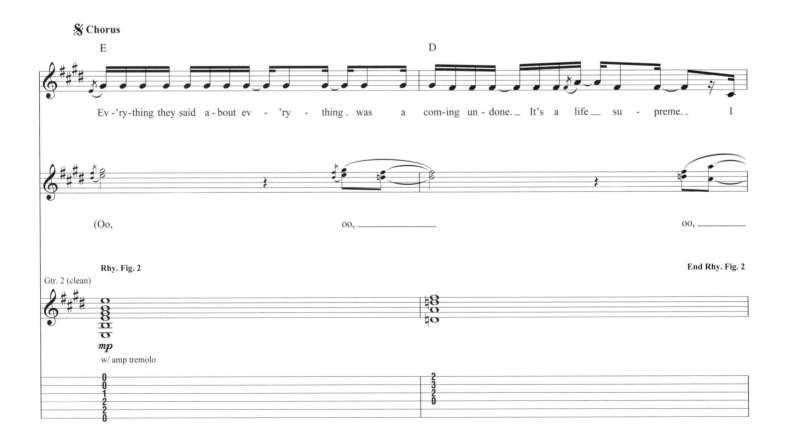

Ev-'ry-thing they said a-bout ev - 'ry - thing ___ was a com-ing un-done. ___ It's a life ___ su - preme. ___ I

(Oo,   oo, ___   (Oo, ___

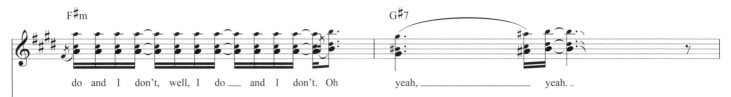

do and I don't, well, I do ___ and I don't. Oh yeah, _____ yeah. _

Voc. Fill 1 End Voc. Fill 1

oo.) _____

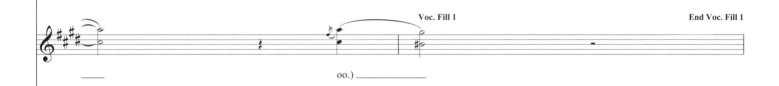

Gtr. 3

Gtr. 4

Rhy. Fill 1A End Rhy. Fill 1A

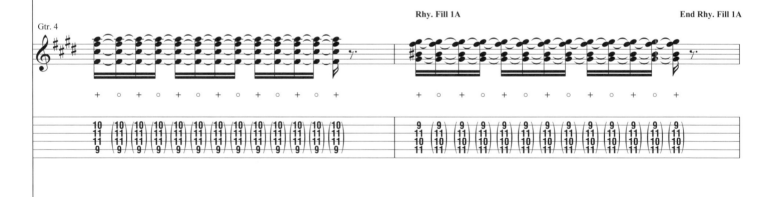

Rhy. Fill 1 End Rhy. Fill 1

Gtr. 2

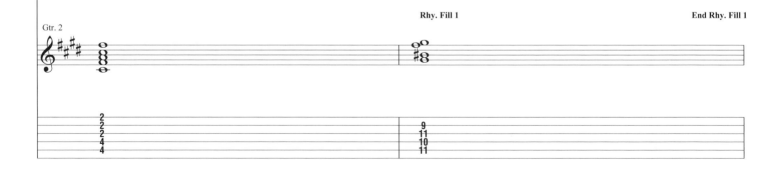

Interlude

Gtr. 2: w/ Rhy. Fill 1

Gtr. 1: w/ Rhy. Fig. 1
Gtrs. 3 & 4 tacet

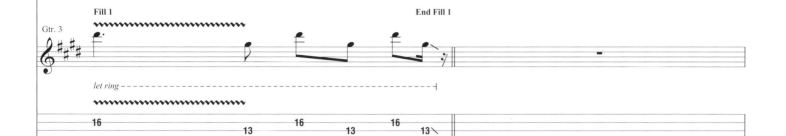

The next di - men - sion, show me in. ___

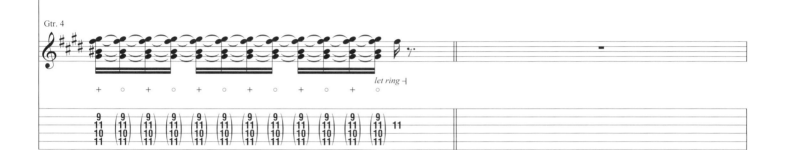

Verse

Gtr. 1: w/ Riff A (2 times)

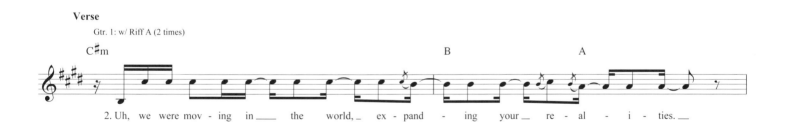

2. Uh, we were mov - ing in ___ the world, ex - pand - ing your re - al - i - ties. ___

A force of na - ture on ___ the verge, ___ com - mand - ing ab - nor - mal - i - ties. ___ Uh,

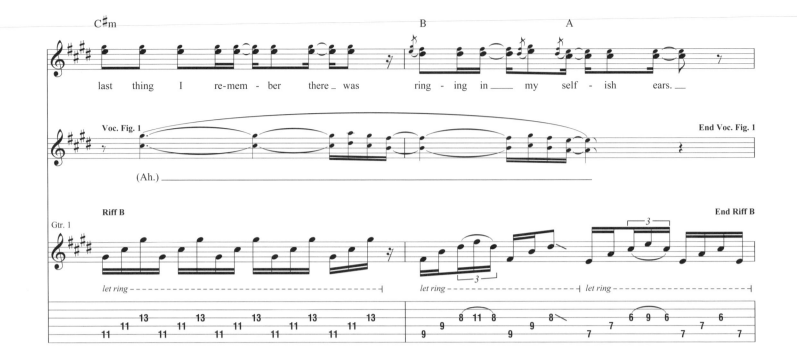

last thing I re-mem-ber there was ring-ing in my self-ish ears.

(Ah.)

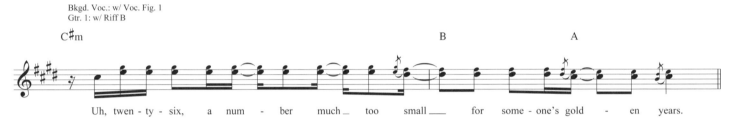

D.S. al Coda 1

Bkgd. Voc.: w/ Voc. Fig. 1
Gtr. 1: w/ Riff B

Uh, twen-ty-six, a num - ber much too small for some-one's gold - en years.

⊕ Coda 1

Interlude

Gtrs. 2 & 4: w/ Rhy. Fills 1 & 1A
Gtr. 3: w/ Fill 1

The next di-men - sion, show me in.

*Set for one octave above.

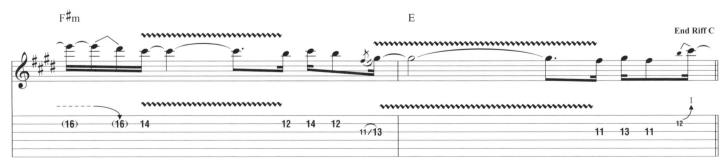

Bridge

Gtr. 5: w/ Riff C (1 1/2 times)

You get a lit - tle bit __ more this time __ when you give a lit - tle bit for your broth-er's kind. __

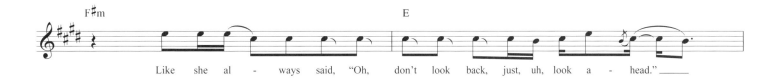

Like she al - ways said, "Oh, don't look back, just, uh, look a - head." _____

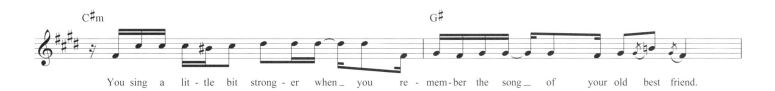

You sing a lit - tle bit strong - er when __ you re - mem - ber the song __ of your old best friend.

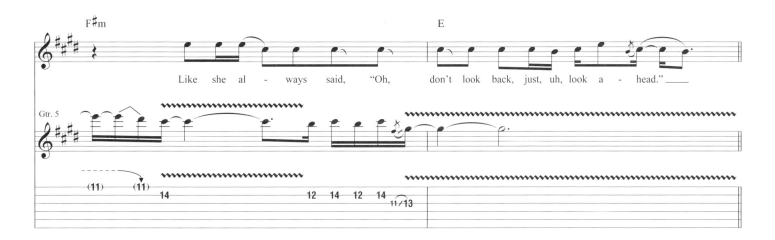

Like she al - ways said, "Oh, don't look back, just, uh, look a - head." _____

Gtr. 5

D.S. al Coda 2

Interlude

Gtr. 1: w/ Rhy. Fig. 1
Gtr. 5 tacet

✦ **Coda 2**

Bkgd. Vocs.: w/ Voc. Fill 1
Gtrs. 2 & 4: w/ Rhy. Fills 1 & 1A

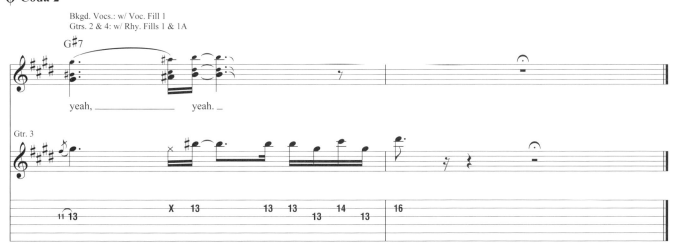

yeah, _____ yeah. __

Gtr. 3

Detroit

Words and Music by Anthony Kiedis, Flea, Chad Smith and Josh Klinghoffer

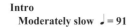

Intro
Moderately slow ♩ = 91

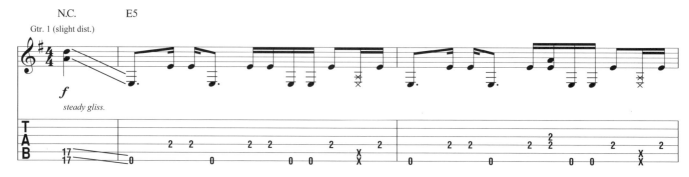

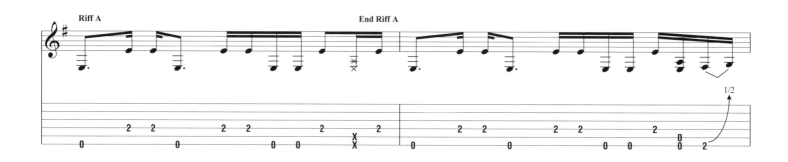

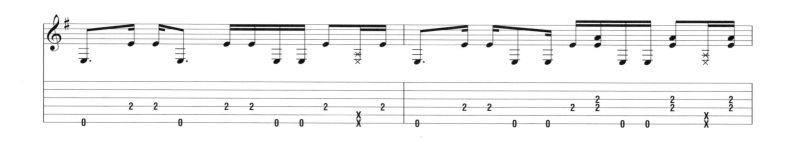

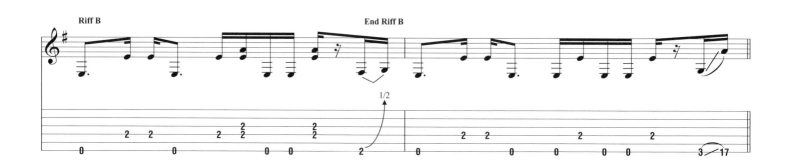

Verse

Gtr. 1: w/ Riff A (2 times)

E5

1. Find me in the sub - urbs and _____ the

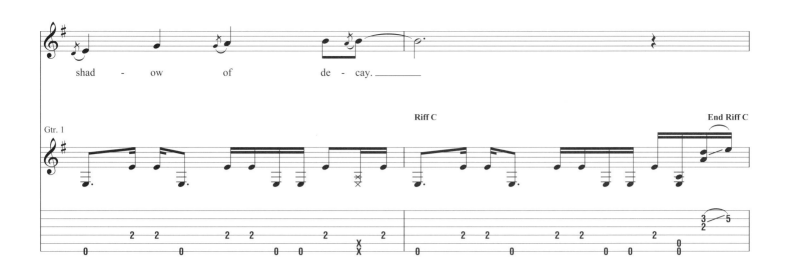

shad - ow of de - cay. _____

Gtr. 1: w/ Riff A (3 times)

Roll - ing rings of rub - ber and _____ the

Gtr. 1: w/ Riff B

band be - gins to play. _____

Gtr. 1: w/ Riff A (2 times)

Am I on the right ___ side of the left _____ side of your brain? ____

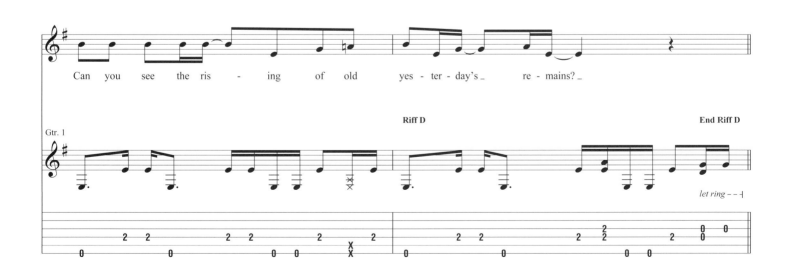

Can you see the ris - ing of old yes - ter - day's _ re - mains? _

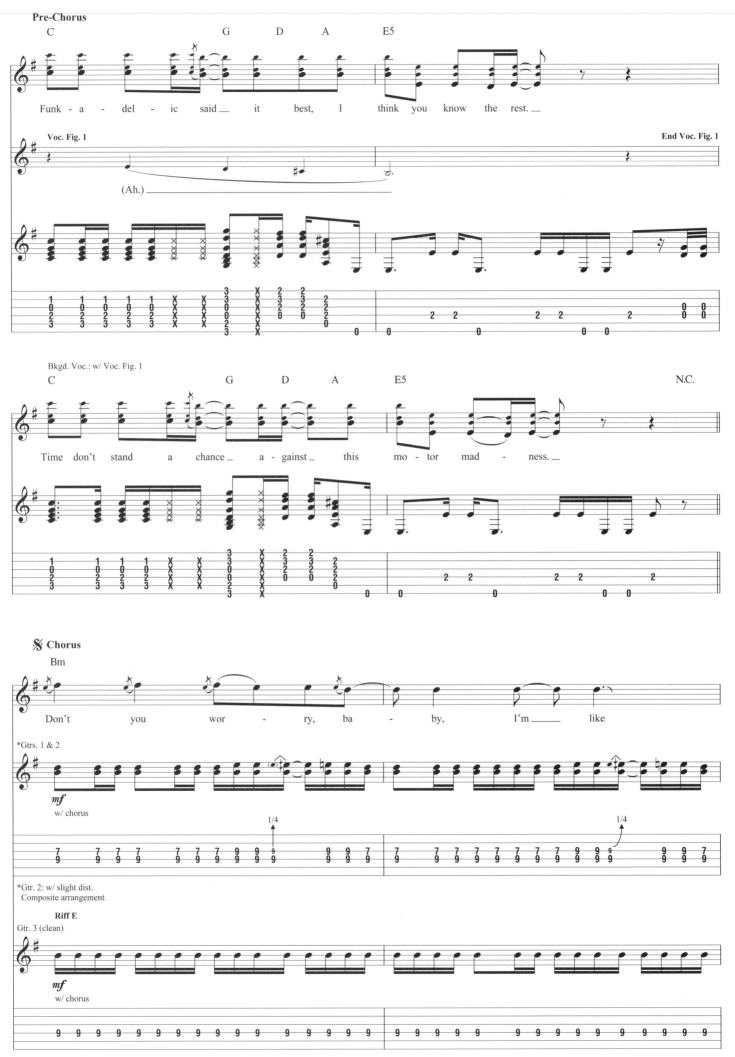

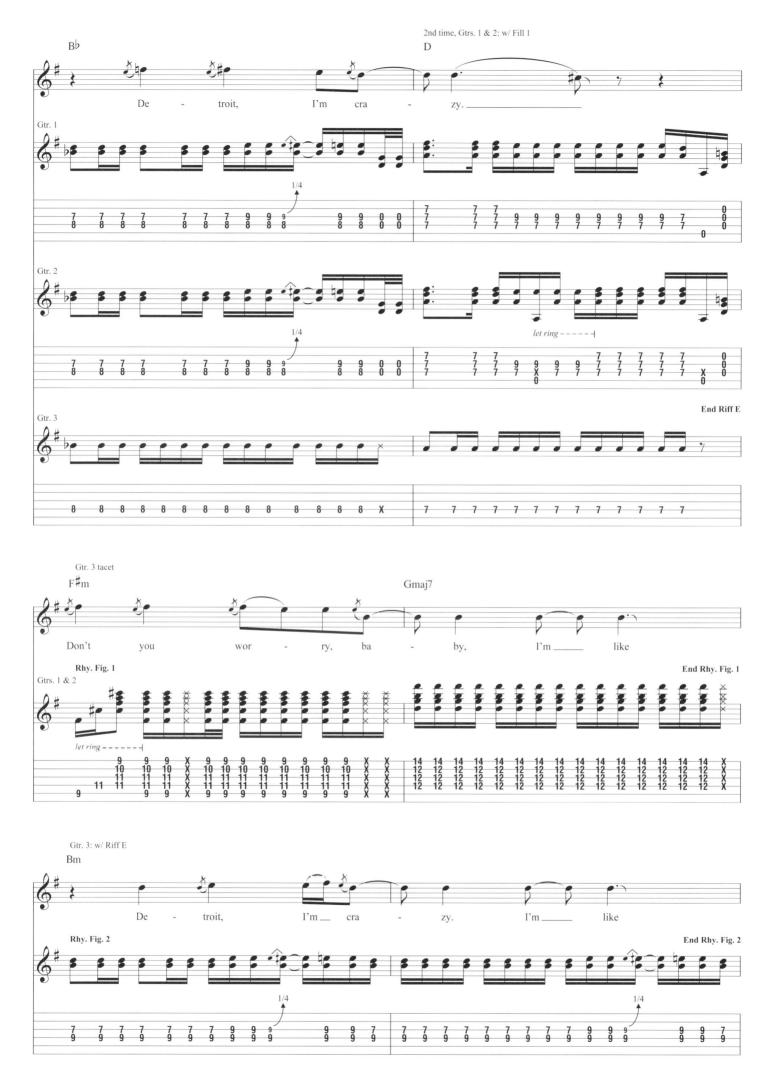

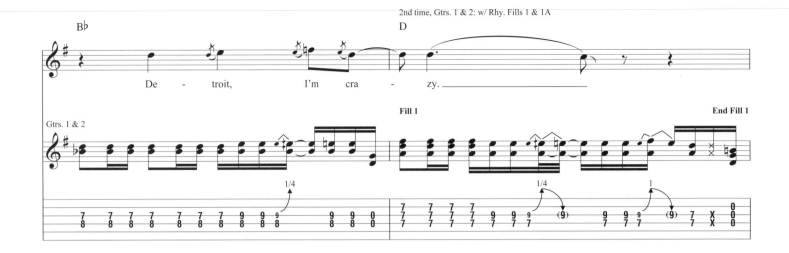

De - troit, I'm cra - zy. _____

To Coda ✛

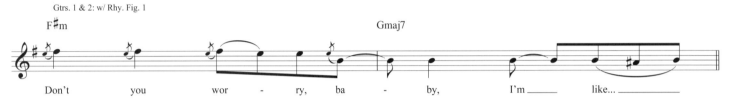

Don't you wor - ry, ba - by, I'm ____ like... ____

Interlude

2. The

Verse

Stoog - es and J Dil - la, yeah, __ they tore this town a - part. _____

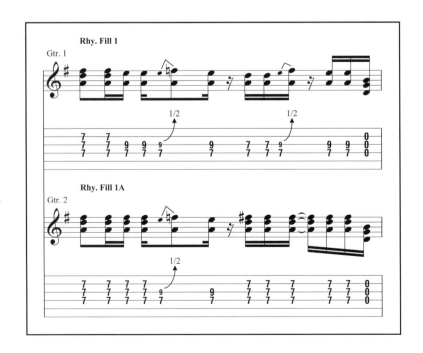

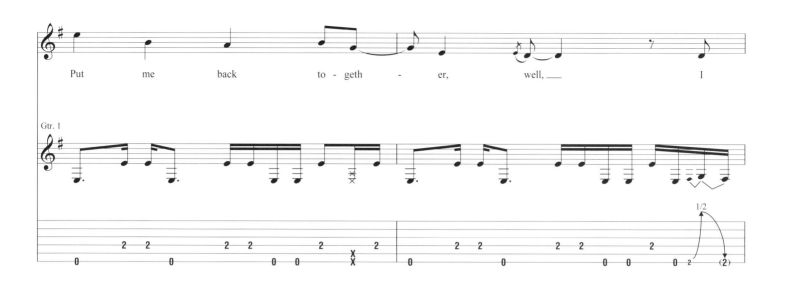

Put me back to-geth - er, well, ___ I

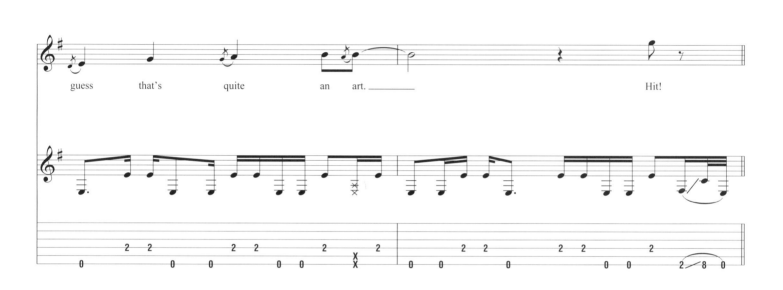

guess that's quite an art. _____ Hit!

Interlude

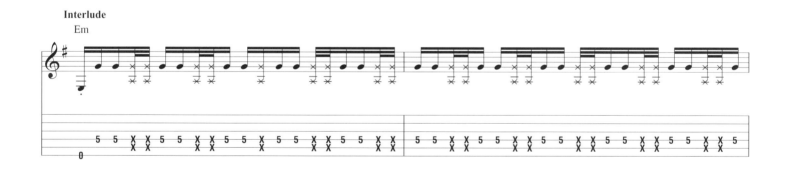

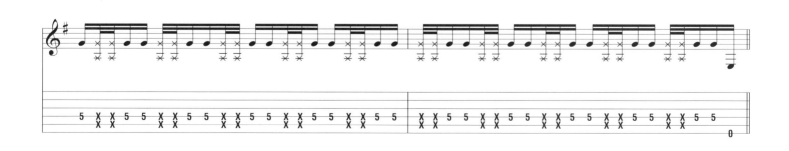

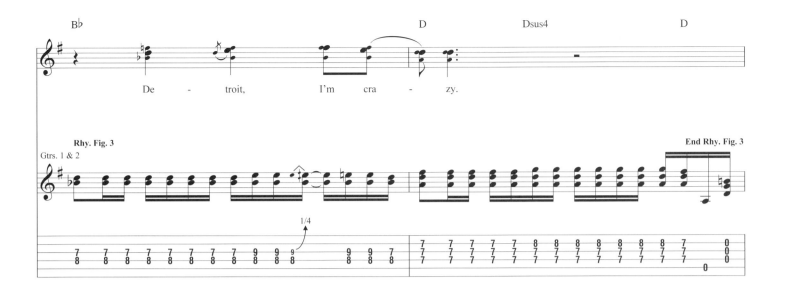

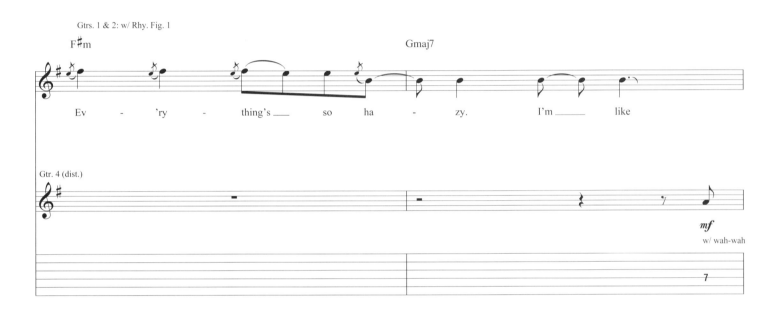

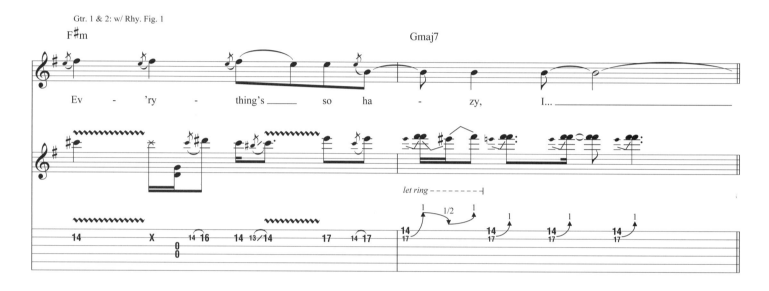

Outro

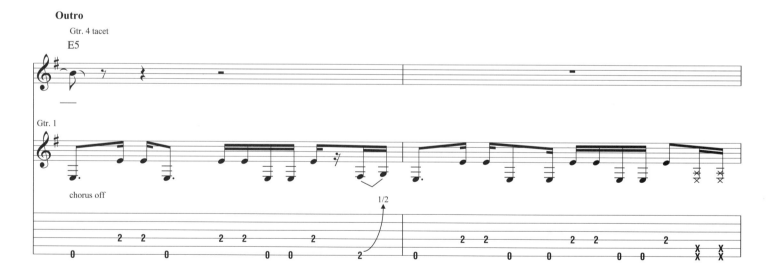

This Ticonderoga

Words and Music by Anthony Kiedis, Flea, Chad Smith and Josh Klinghoffer

join the la - zy zoo? All these hu - man but - ter - flies and cac - tus flow - ers, swol - len eyes. And

I want the dev - il's share _ of you, I do _ de - clare. A - gain I'm ask - ing, can I do when

D.S.S. al Coda 2

Gtr. 3 tacet

all these an - i - mals want to be just like you?

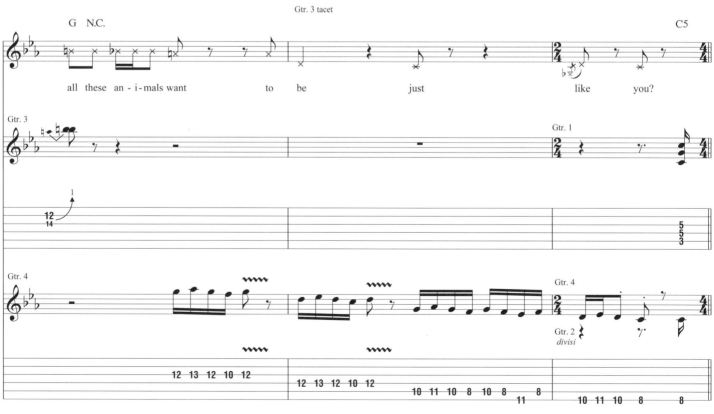

Encore

Words and Music by Anthony Kiedis, Flea, Chad Smith and Josh Klinghoffer

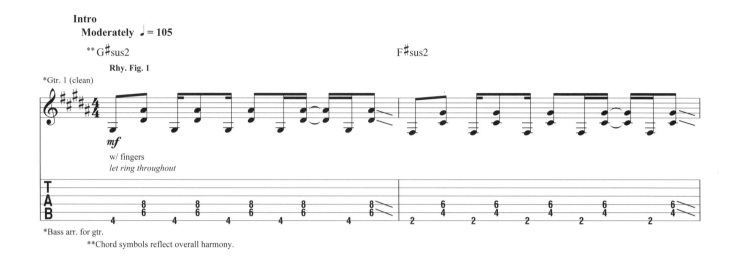

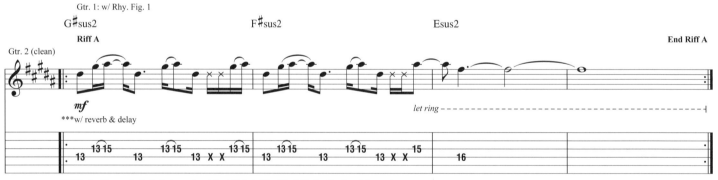

***Electro-Harmonix Cathedral reverb, set for infinite hold, w/ EarthQuaker Devices Afterneath.

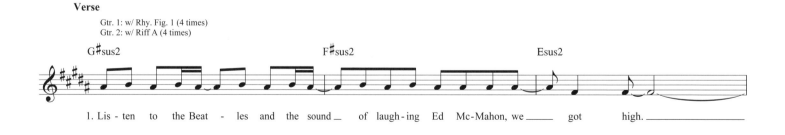

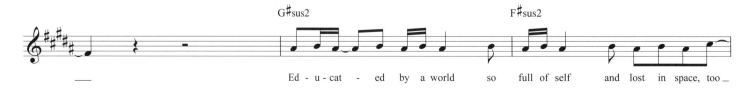

much pride. ___ Cos - mo - nauts ___ and dirt - y thoughts ___ are

jug - gl - ing ___ the jug - ger - naut, So - vi - et Spy. ___

Ev - 'ry now ___ and then when I ___ re - mem - ber to ___ be - friend the lit - tle things ___

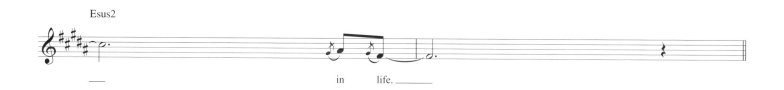

___ in life. ___

Chorus

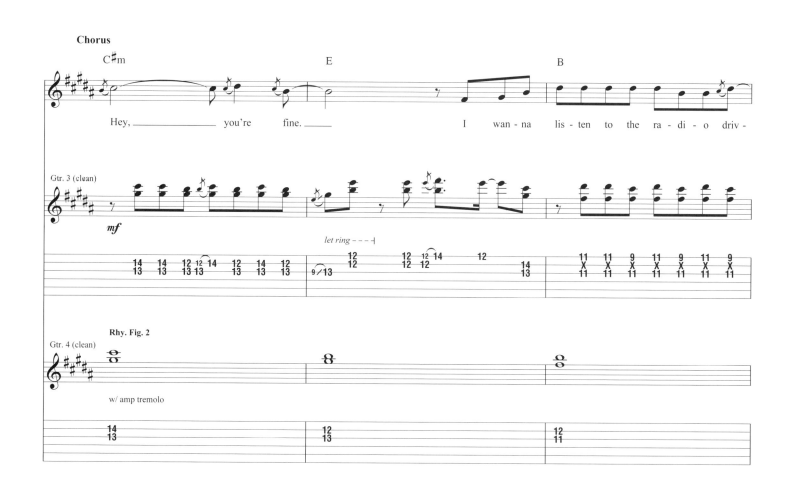

Hey, ___ you're fine. ___ I wan - na lis - ten to the ra - di - o driv -

-ing down Ca - lex - i - co high - way. And now I know the signs

let ring *let ring*

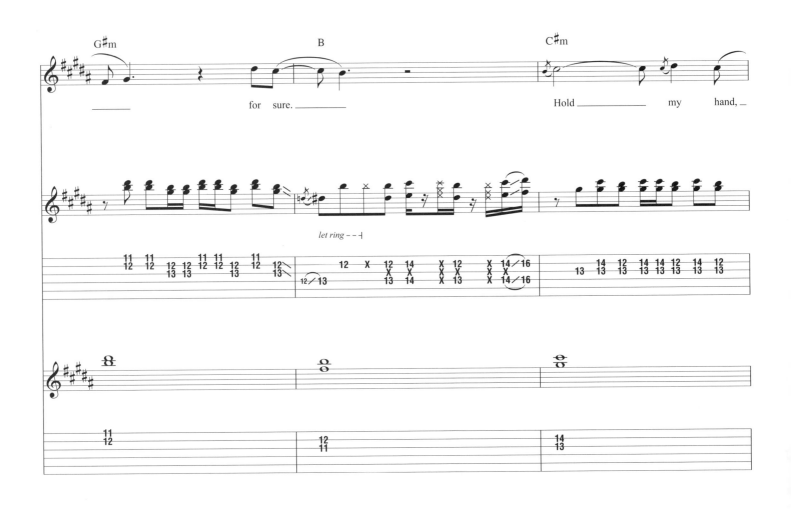

for sure. Hold my hand,

let ring

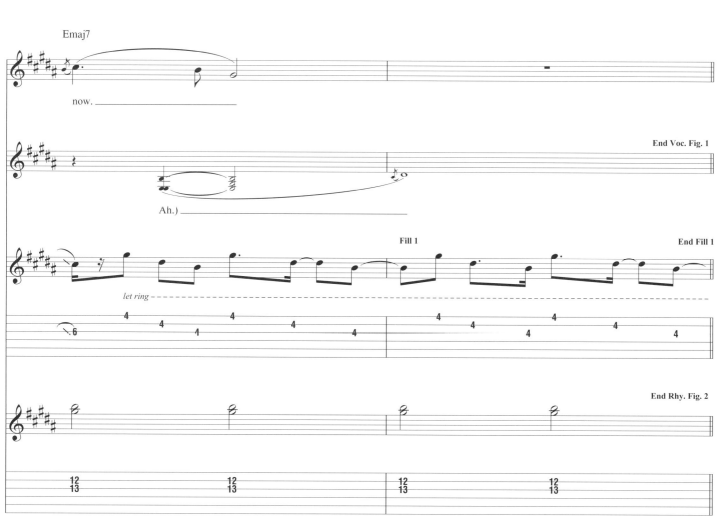

Verse

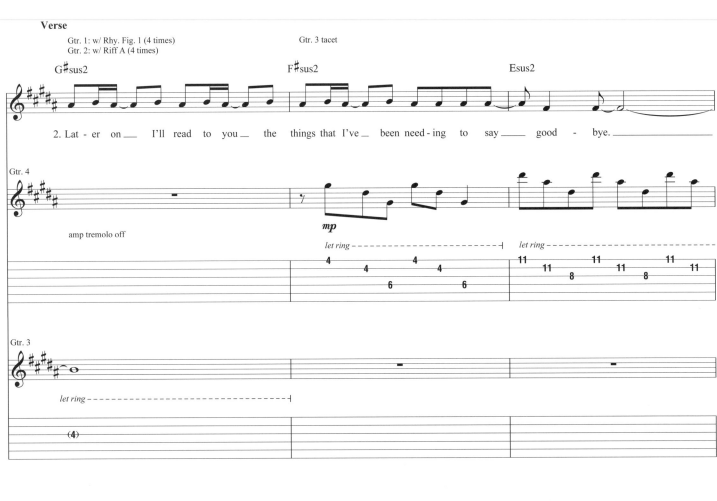

2. Lat-er on ___ I'll read to you ___ the things that I've ___ been need-ing to say ___ good - bye. _____

Walk a - way ___ from mom and dad ___ to find the love ___ you nev - er had, tell ___

no lies. ___ Car - ry on ___ and write a song ___ that

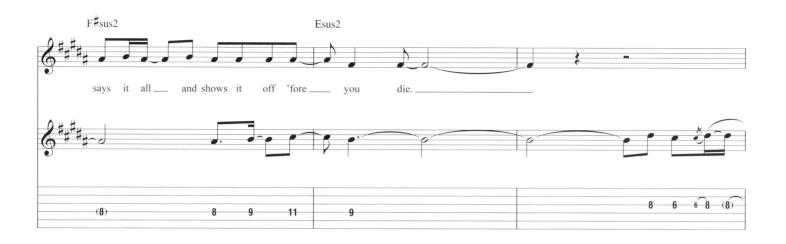

Chorus

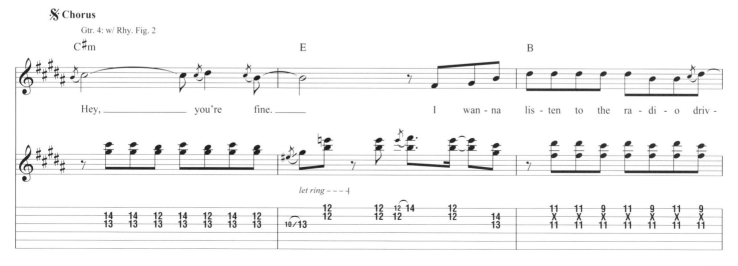

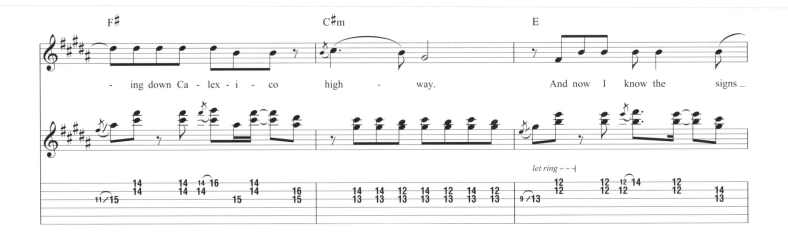

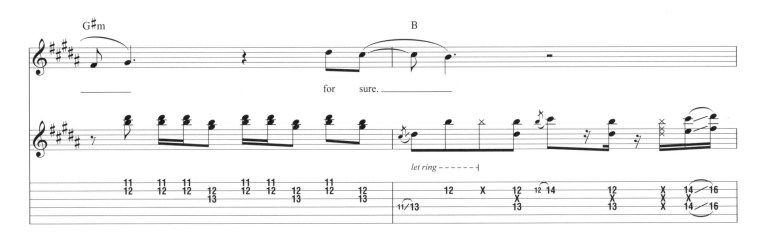

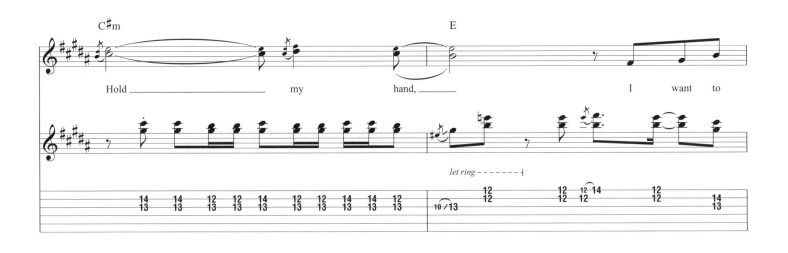

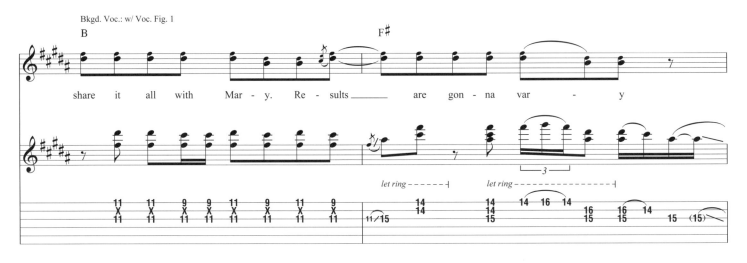

2nd time, Gtr. 3: w/ Fill 1

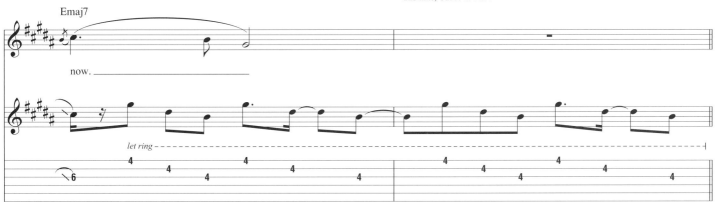

Interlude

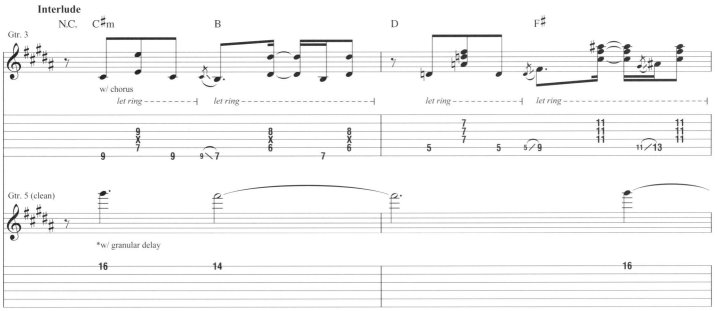

*Red Panda Particle Granular delay pedal.

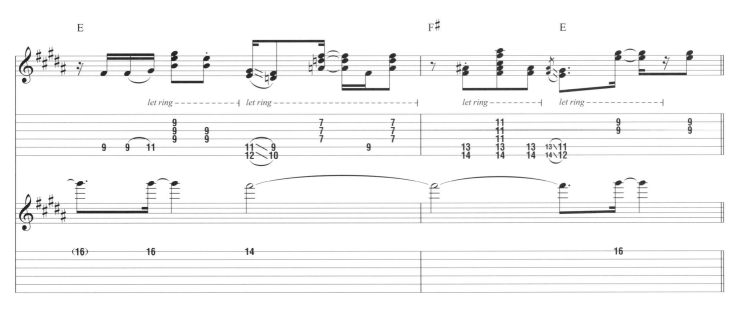

Verse

Gtr. 1: w/ Rhy. Fig. 1 (2 times)
Gtr. 2: w/ Riff A (2 times)
Gtrs. 3 & 5 tacet

3. Skin-ny brains and lit-tle stains up - on your face. Teen-age re - mains tell ___ me more. ___

Lift - ed in the fif - ties when you re-al-ly ra - ther drift - ed through time,

D.S. al Coda

let's soar.

Coda
Outro

Begin fade

Fade out

The Hunter

Words and Music by Anthony Kiedis, Flea, Chad Smith, Josh Klinghoffer and Brian Burton

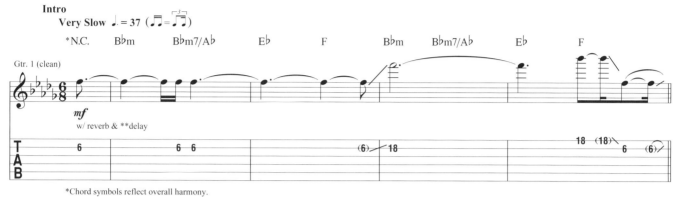

*Chord symbols reflect overall harmony.

**Boss DD-6 on warp setting.

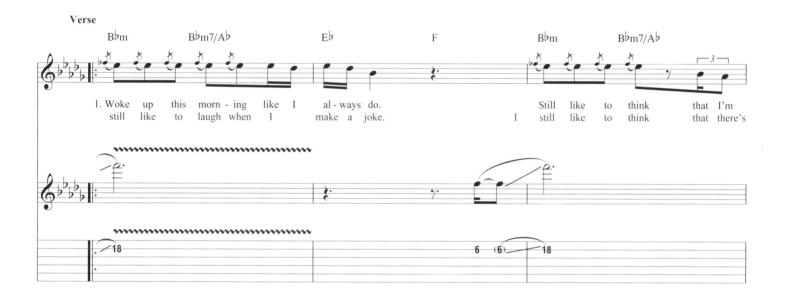

1. Woke up this morn-ing like I al-ways do.
still like to laugh when I make a joke.

Still like to think that I'm
I still like to think that there's

new.
hope.

Time just gets its ___ way; ___
Time ___ just has its ___ say; ___

*Set for eighth-note regeneration w/ 15 repeats.

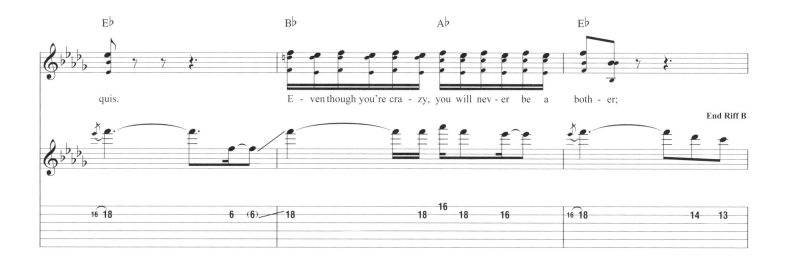

quis.

E - ven though you're cra - zy, you will nev - er be a both - er;

End Riff B

1.

2.

you're my Old Man in the Sea.

3. I Sea.

(Oo.

delay off

Interlude

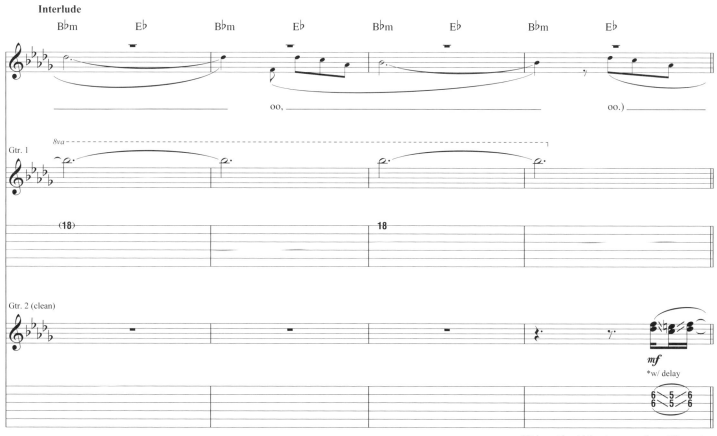

oo,

oo.)

Gtr. 1

Gtr. 2 (clean)

mf

*w/ delay

*Delay set for eighth-note regeneration w/ 12 repeats.

Dreams of a Samurai

Words and Music by Anthony Kiedis, Flea, Chad Smith and Josh Klinghoffer

Gtrs. 3 & 4: Drop D tuning:
(low to high) D-A-D-G-B-E

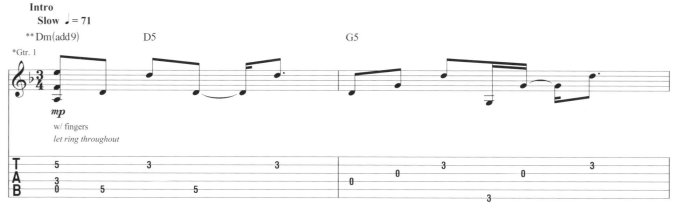

*Piano arr. for gtr.

  **Chord symbols reflect overall harmony.

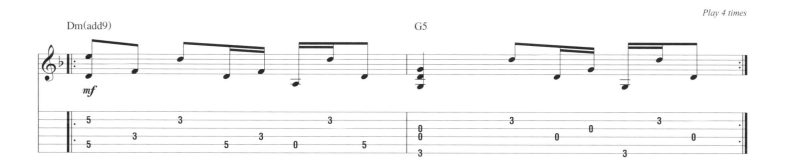

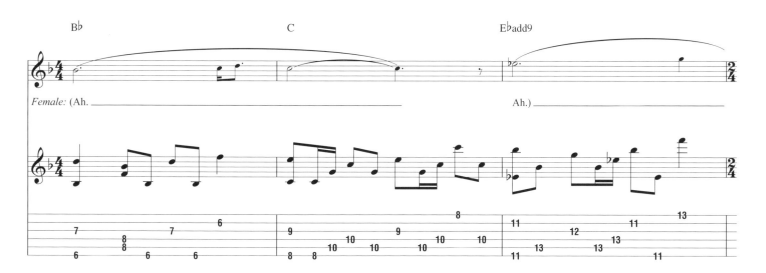

Gtr. 1 tacet

Gm   Cadd9   Dm7   G5

Dm7   G5   Dm7   G5   Dm7   G5

Gtr. 2 (clean)

mp

w/ wah-wah & delay

string noise   string noise - - - -

Delay set for eighth-note regeneration w/ 4 repeats.

Verse

Dm7   G5   Dm7   G5

1. Stand - ing na - ked in your kitch - en, ___   feel - ing free ___ that I could be a - live. ___

delay off

Dm7   G5   Dm7   G5

Clear - ly I'm ___ a con-tra-dic - tion, ___   too young to be ___ my wife.

steady gliss. ⌐

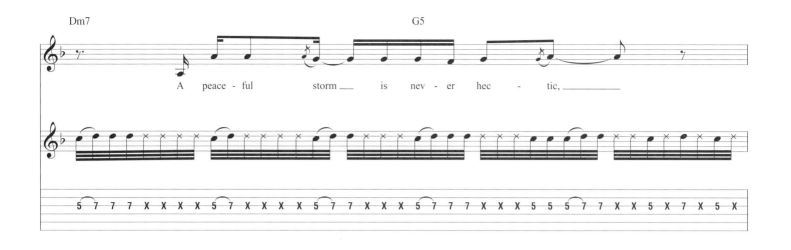

A peace-ful storm ___ is nev-er hec ___ -tic, ___

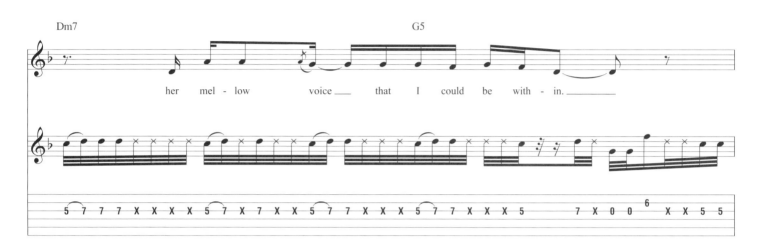

her mel-low voice ___ that I could be with - in. ___

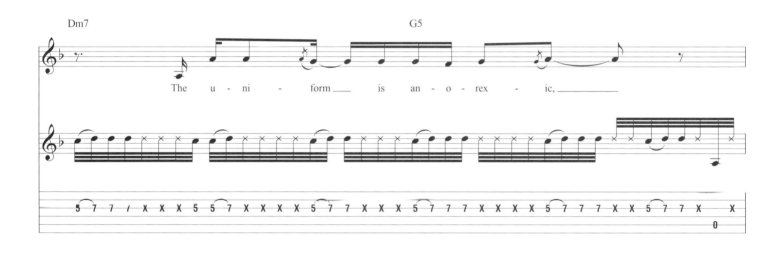

The u-ni - form ___ is an-o-rex - ic, ___

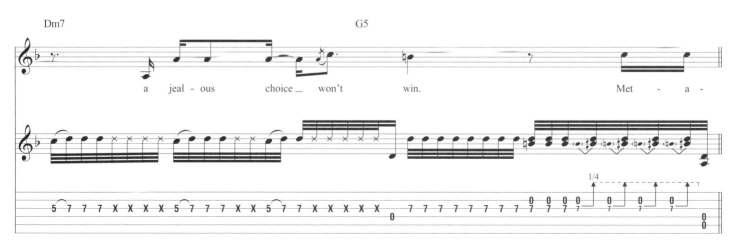

a jeal-ous choice ___ won't win. Met - a-

Pre-Chorus

Gtr. 2 tacet

mor - pho-sis sam-u - rai. You got a lit-tle lord fish and I don't know why ___ I got a met-a-

*Gtrs. 3 & 4 (dist.)

mf

**w/ wah-wah & heavy reverb

let ring

*Composite arrangement

**Wah-wah used as filter.

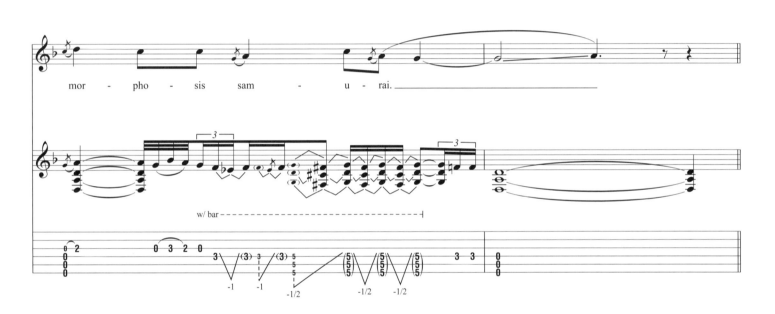

mor - pho - sis sam - u - rai. _____

w/ bar

Verse

Gtrs. 3 & 4 tacet

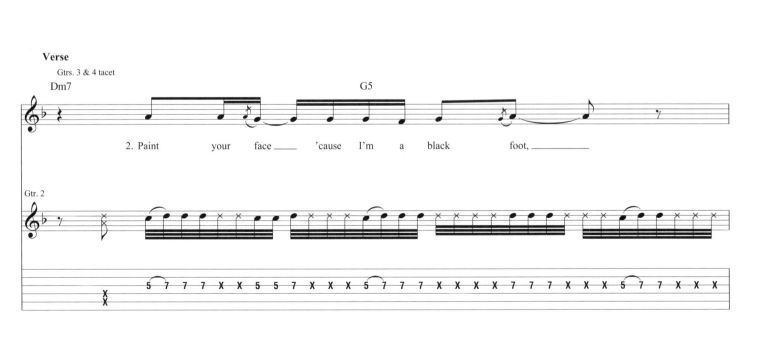

2. Paint your face ___ 'cause I'm a black foot, _____

Gtr. 2

I thought I count - ed up the fire - flies. _____

Close e - nough ___ to get a good look,

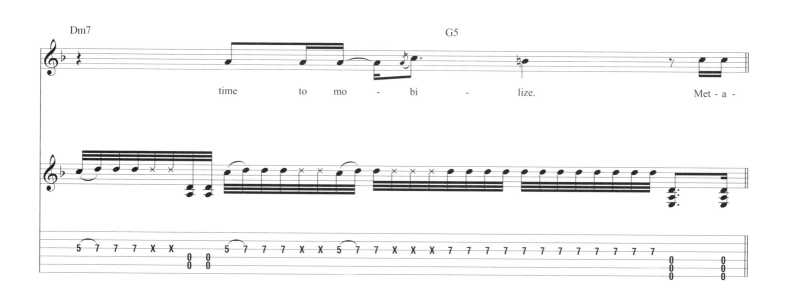

time to mo - bi - lize. Met - a -

Pre-Chorus

Gtr. 2 tacet

mor - pho - sis sam-u - rai. ___ You got a lit - tle lord fish and I don't know why ___ I got a met-a-

*Composite arrangement

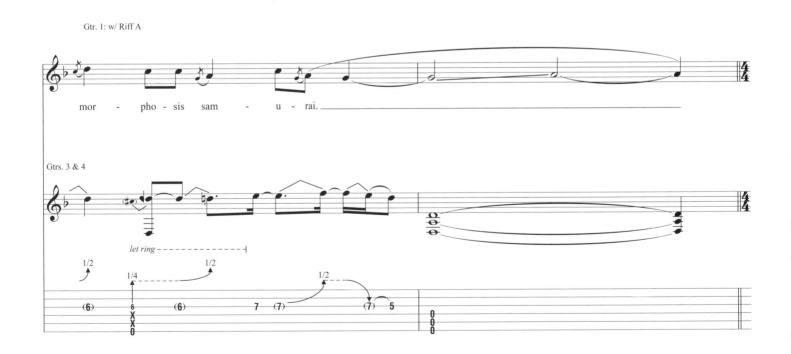

mor - pho - sis sam - u - rai. ___

Verse

Gtr. 1: w/ Riff A (4 times)
Gtrs. 3, 4 & 5 tacet

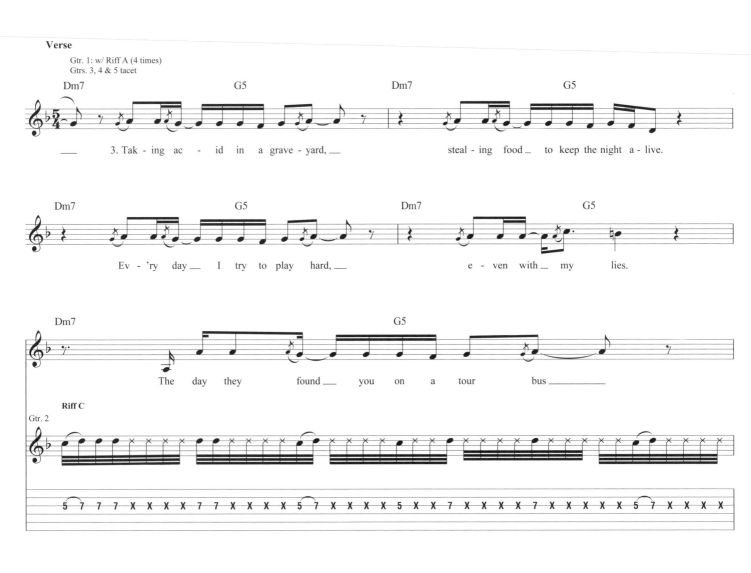

___ 3. Tak - ing ac - id in a grave - yard, ___ steal - ing food ___ to keep the night a - live.

Ev - 'ry day ___ I try to play hard, ___ e - ven with ___ my lies.

The day they found ___ you on a tour bus ___

Riff C

Gtr. 2

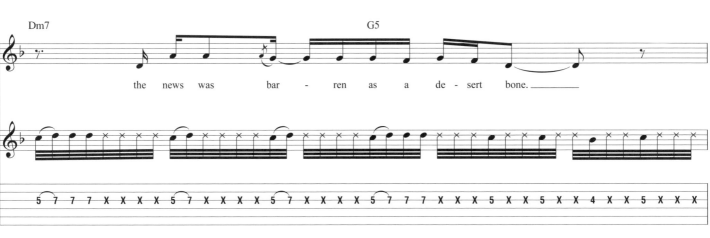

the news was bar - ren as a de - sert bone. ___

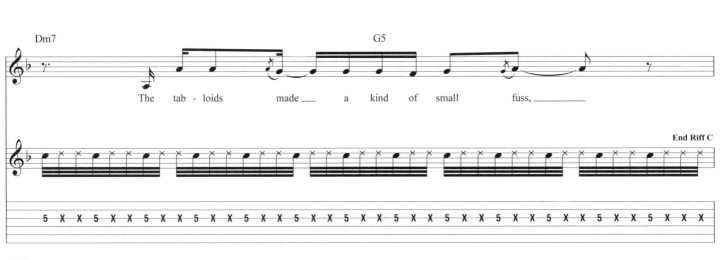

The tab - loids made ___ a kind of small fuss, ___

End Riff C

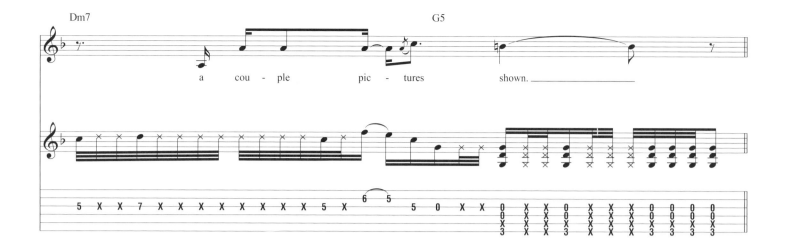

a cou - ple pic - tures shown.

Interlude

Gtr. 1: w/ Riff A (2 times)
Gtr. 2 tacet

Dm7

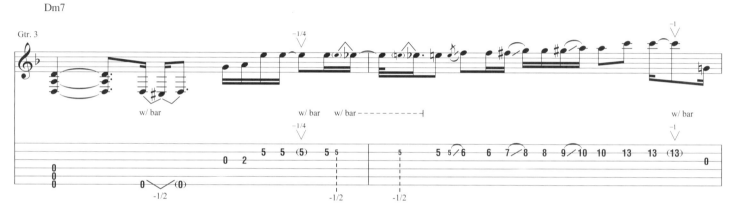

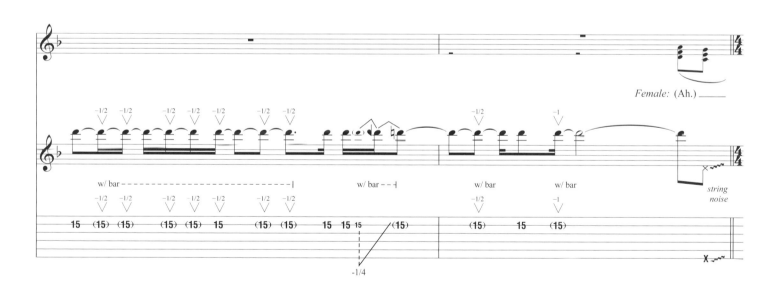

Female: (Ah.)

string noise

Chorus

Bkgd. Voc.: w/ Voc. Fig. 1
Gtrs. 3 & 4: w/ Rhy. Fig. 1
Gtr. 5: w/ Riff B

I'm a lone - ly lad, __ I've lost my-self out on the range. __

I don't re-mem - ber much, _ so don't ask me. I've gone in - sane. _____

Interlude

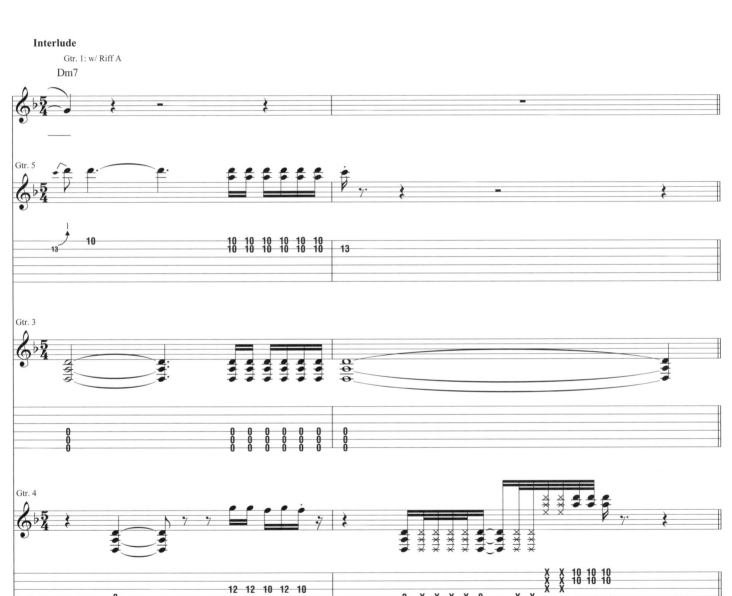

Gtr. 1: w/ Riff A

Dm7

Gtr. 5

Gtr. 3

Gtr. 4

Verse

Gtr. 1: w/ Riff A (4 times)
Gtr. 2: w/ Riff C
Gtrs. 3, 4 & 5 tacet

Dm7   G5   Dm7   G5

4. Slow - ly turn - ing in - to drift - wood, _ no one ev - er wants to die a - lone. __

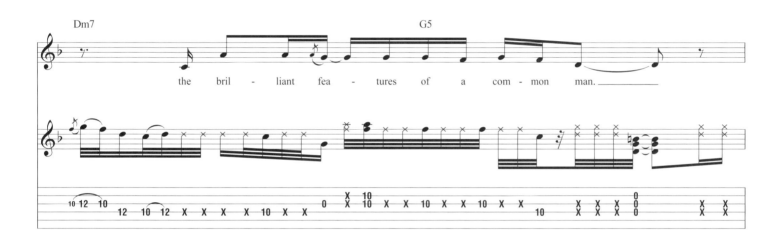

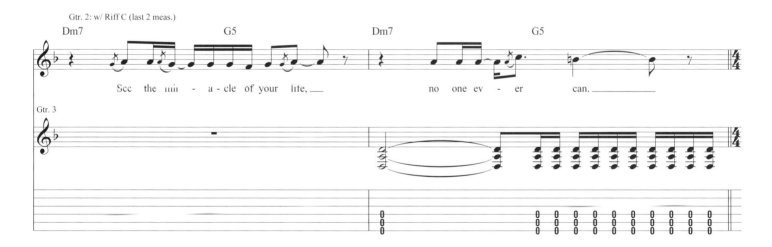

Chorus

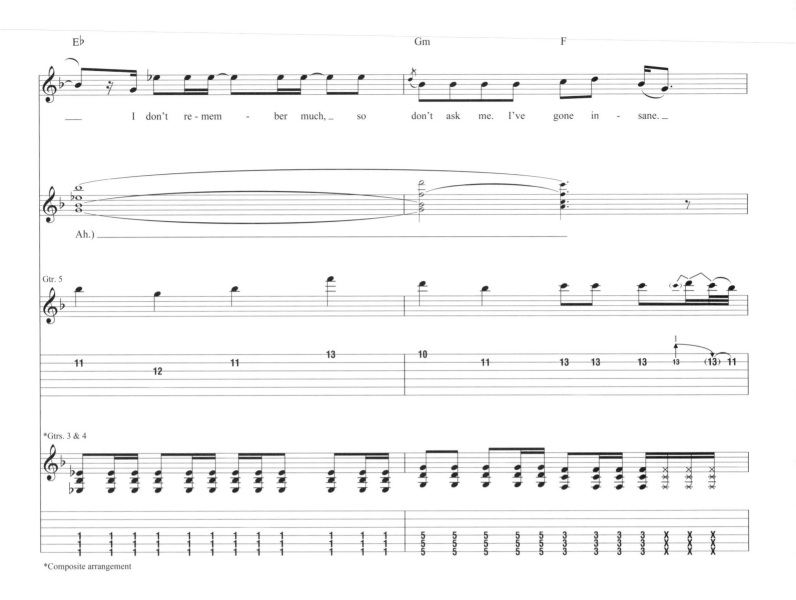

I don't re-mem - ber much, _ so don't ask me. I've gone in - sane. _

Ah.) ___

Gtr. 5

*Gtrs. 3 & 4

*Composite arrangement

Bkgd. Voc.: w/ Voc. Fig. 1

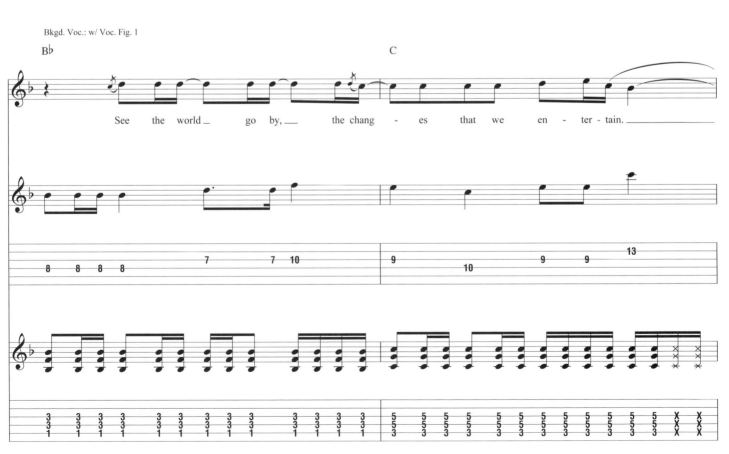

See the world _ go by, _ the chang - es that we en - ter - tain. _

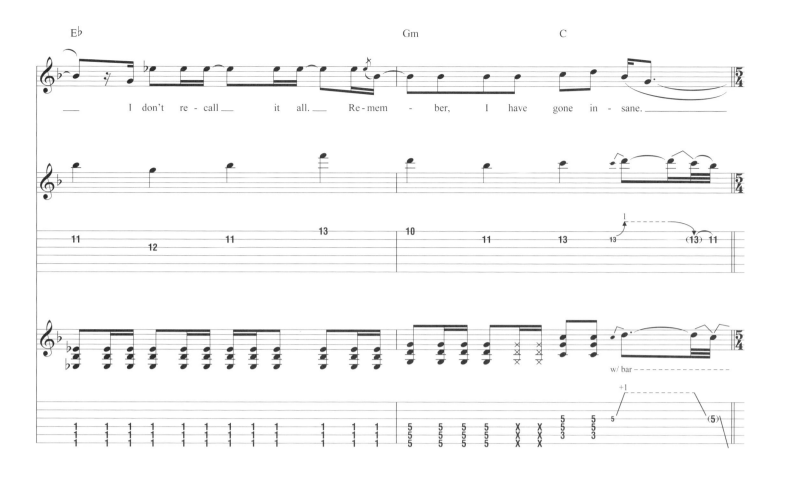

Interlude

Gtr. 1: w/ Riff A (2 times)

Gtrs. 3 & 4 tacet

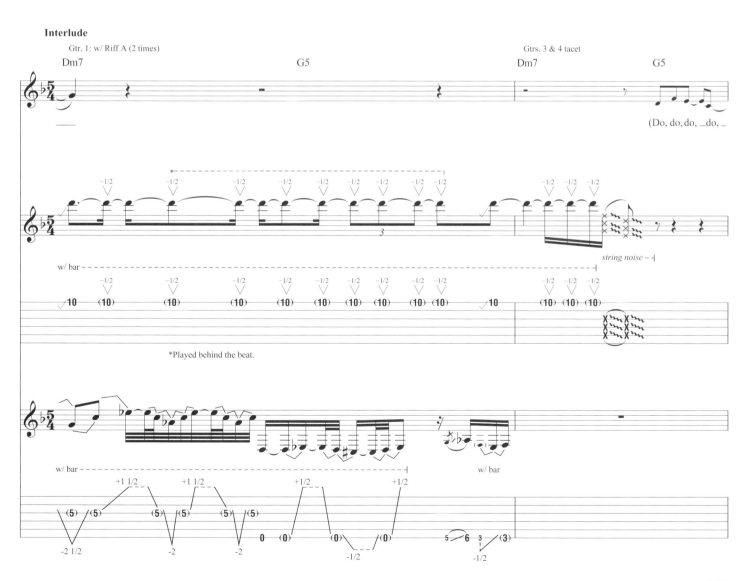

*Played behind the beat.

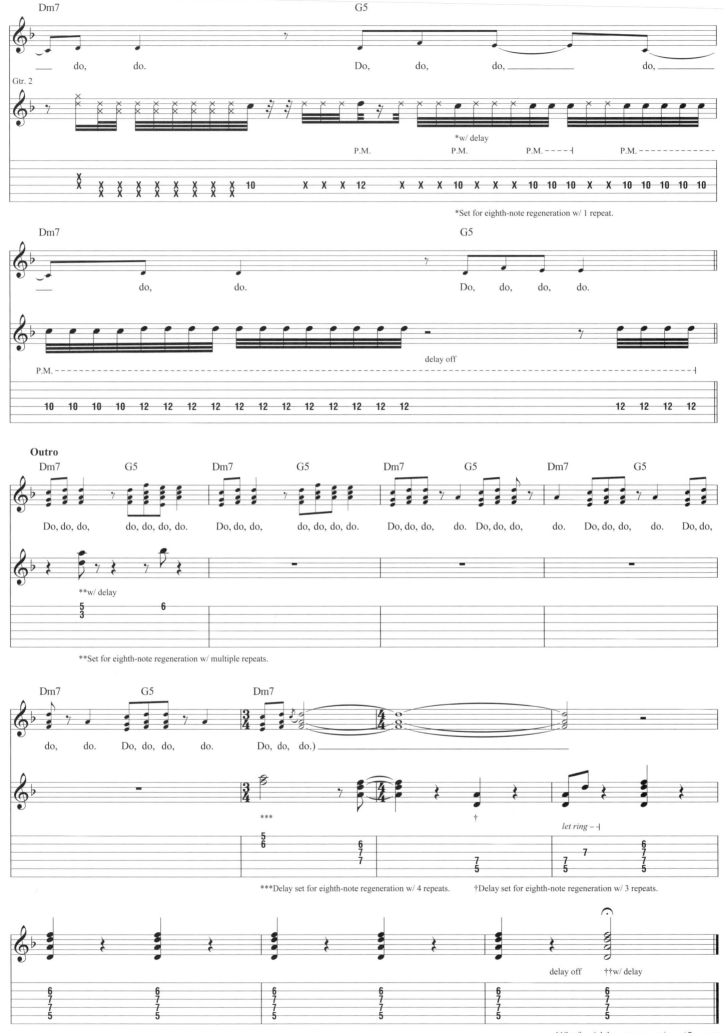

*Set for eighth-note regeneration w/ 1 repeat.

**Set for eighth-note regeneration w/ multiple repeats.

***Delay set for eighth-note regeneration w/ 4 repeats.   †Delay set for eighth-note regeneration w/ 3 repeats.

††Set for eighth-note regeneration w/ 7 repeats.

GUITAR NOTATION LEGEND

Guitar music can be notated three different ways: on a *musical staff*, in *tablature*, and in *rhythm slashes*.

RHYTHM SLASHES are written above the staff. Strum chords in the rhythm indicated. Use the chord diagrams found at the top of the first page of the transcription for the appropriate chord voicings. Round noteheads indicate single notes.

THE MUSICAL STAFF shows pitches and rhythms and is divided by bar lines into measures. Pitches are named after the first seven letters of the alphabet.

TABLATURE graphically represents the guitar fingerboard. Each horizontal line represents a string, and each number represents a fret.

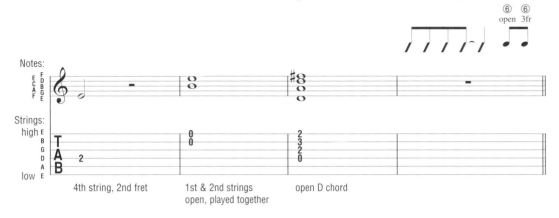

4th string, 2nd fret | 1st & 2nd strings open, played together | open D chord

Definitions for Special Guitar Notation

HALF-STEP BEND: Strike the note and bend up 1/2 step.

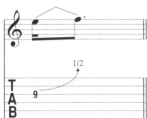

WHOLE-STEP BEND: Strike the note and bend up one step.

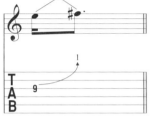

GRACE NOTE BEND: Strike the note and immediately bend up as indicated.

SLIGHT (MICROTONE) BEND: Strike the note and bend up 1/4 step.

BEND AND RELEASE: Strike the note and bend up as indicated, then release back to the original note. Only the first note is struck.

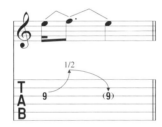

PRE-BEND: Bend the note as indicated, then strike it.

PRE-BEND AND RELEASE: Bend the note as indicated. Strike it and release the bend back to the original note.

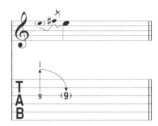

UNISON BEND: Strike the two notes simultaneously and bend the lower note up to the pitch of the higher.

VIBRATO: The string is vibrated by rapidly bending and releasing the note with the fretting hand.

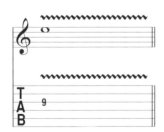

WIDE VIBRATO: The pitch is varied to a greater degree by vibrating with the fretting hand.

HAMMER-ON: Strike the first (lower) note with one finger, then sound the higher note (on the same string) with another finger by fretting it without picking.

PULL-OFF: Place both fingers on the notes to be sounded. Strike the first note and without picking, pull the finger off to sound the second (lower) note.

LEGATO SLIDE: Strike the first note and then slide the same fret-hand finger up or down to the second note. The second note is not struck.

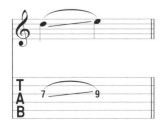

SHIFT SLIDE: Same as legato slide, except the second note is struck.

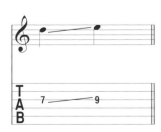

TRILL: Very rapidly alternate between the notes indicated by continuously hammering on and pulling off.

TAPPING: Hammer ("tap") the fret indicated with the pick-hand index or middle finger and pull off to the note fretted by the fret hand.

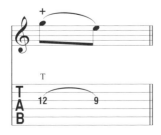

NATURAL HARMONIC: Strike the note while the fret-hand lightly touches the string directly over the fret indicated.

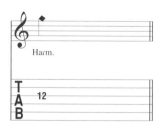

PINCH HARMONIC: The note is fretted normally and a harmonic is produced by adding the edge of the thumb or the tip of the index finger of the pick hand to the normal pick attack.

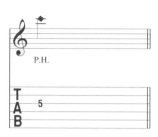

HARP HARMONIC: The note is fretted normally and a harmonic is produced by gently resting the pick hand's index finger directly above the indicated fret (in parentheses) while the pick hand's thumb or pick assists by plucking the appropriate string.

PICK SCRAPE: The edge of the pick is rubbed down (or up) the string, producing a scratchy sound.

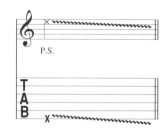

MUFFLED STRINGS: A percussive sound is produced by laying the fret hand across the string(s) without depressing, and striking them with the pick hand.

PALM MUTING: The note is partially muted by the pick hand lightly touching the string(s) just before the bridge.

RAKE: Drag the pick across the strings indicated with a single motion.

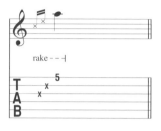

TREMOLO PICKING: The note is picked as rapidly and continuously as possible.

ARPEGGIATE: Play the notes of the chord indicated by quickly rolling them from bottom to top.

VIBRATO BAR DIVE AND RETURN: The pitch of the note or chord is dropped a specified number of steps (in rhythm), then returned to the original pitch.

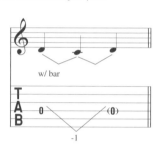

VIBRATO BAR SCOOP: Depress the bar just before striking the note, then quickly release the bar.

VIBRATO BAR DIP: Strike the note and then immediately drop a specified number of steps, then release back to the original pitch.

Additional Musical Definitions

(accent) • Accentuate note (play it louder).

(accent) • Accentuate note with great intensity.

(staccato) • Play the note short.

⊓ • Downstroke

V • Upstroke

D.S. al Coda • Go back to the sign (𝄋), then play until the measure marked "*To Coda*," then skip to the section labelled "**Coda**."

D.C. al Fine • Go back to the beginning of the song and play until the measure marked "*Fine*" (end).

Rhy. Fig. • Label used to recall a recurring accompaniment pattern (usually chordal).

Riff • Label used to recall composed, melodic lines (usually single notes) which recur.

Fill • Label used to identify a brief melodic figure which is to be inserted into the arrangement.

Rhy. Fill • A chordal version of a Fill.

tacet • Instrument is silent (drops out).

• Repeat measures between signs.

• When a repeated section has different endings, play the first ending only the first time and the second ending only the second time.

NOTE: Tablature numbers in parentheses mean:
1. The note is being sustained over a system (note in standard notation is tied), or
2. The note is sustained, but a new articulation (such as a hammer-on, pull-off, slide or vibrato) begins, or
3. The note is a barely audible "ghost" note (note in standard notation is also in parentheses).

TAB+

Accurate Tabs
Gear Information
Selected Pedal Settings
Analysis & Playing Tips

The Tab+ Series gives you note-for-note accurate transcriptions in notes and tab PLUS a whole lot more. These books also include performance notes to help you master the song, tips on the essential gear to make the song sound its best, recording techniques, historical information, right- and left-hand techniques and other playing tips – it's all here!

TAB. TONE. TECHNIQUE.

25 TOP ACOUSTIC SONGS
Big Yellow Taxi • Cat's in the Cradle • Free Fallin' • Going to California • Good Riddance (Time of Your Life) • Hey There Delilah • I Got a Name • Into the Mystic • Lola • Ooh La La • Patience • The Weight • Wild Horses • Wish You Were Here • and more.
00109283..$19.99

25 TOP BLUES SONGS
Baby, Scratch My Back • Down Home Blues • Going Down • I'm Yours and I'm Hers • Reconsider Baby • Right Place, Wrong Time • Shelter Me • Sweet Sixteen • Texas Flood • and more.
00117059..$19.99

25 TOP BLUES/ROCK SONGS
Crossfire • Going Down • Lie to Me • Moonchild • One Way Out • Rock N Roll Susie • True Lies • Twice As Hard • and more.
00122436..$19.99

25 TOP CLASSIC ROCK SONGS
Addicted to Love • Beat It • Brown Sugar • China Grove • Fortunate Son • Life in the Fast Lane • Reeling in the Years • Roundabout • Tom Sawyer • Up on Cripple Creek • Wild Night • and more.
00102519..$19.99

25 TOP HARD ROCK SONGS
Back in Black • Crazy Train • Detroit Rock City • In-A-Gadda-Da-Vida • Jailbreak • Nobody's Fool • Paranoid • Rock Candy • School's Out • Smoke on the Water • Welcome to the Jungle • Whole Lotta Love • Youth Gone Wild • and more.
00102469..$19.99

25 TOP METAL SONGS
Ace of Spades • Afterlife • Blackout • Breaking the Law • Chop Suey! • Evil • Freak on a Leash • Hangar 18 • Iron Man • Mr. Crowley • Psychosocial • Pull Me Under • Sober • Thunder Kiss '65 • The Trooper • Unsung • and more.
00102501..$19.99

25 TOP POST-GRUNGE SONGS
All Star • Boulevard of Broken Dreams • Closing Time • Everlong • Far Behind • I Hate Everything About You • It's Been Awhile • Kryptonite • One Week • The Reason • Remedy • Sex and Candy • Thnks Fr Th Mmrs • and more.
00102518..$19.99

25 TOP ROCK BASS SONGS
Another One Bites the Dust • Blurred Lines • The Boys Are Back in Town • Freewill • Hey Joe • The Joker • London Calling • My Generation • Sledgehammer • Sweet Emotion • Young Lust • and more.
00125929 Bass Recorded Versions $19.99

25 TOP ROCK CLASSICS
Can't You Hear Me Knocking • Cocaine • Fat Bottomed Girls • I Wanna Be Sedated • La Grange • Paradise City • Rebel Yell • Renegade • Simple Man • Sultans of Swing • and more.
00120976..$19.99

HAL•LEONARD® CORPORATION

7777 W. BLUEMOUND RD. P.O. BOX 13819 MILWAUKEE, WI 53213

Prices, contents, and availability subject to change without notice.

www.halleonard.com

0515

GUITAR RECORDED VERSIONS®

Guitar Recorded Versions® are note-for-note transcriptions of guitar music taken directly off recordings. This series, one of the most popular in print today, features some of the greatest guitar players and groups from blues and rock to country and jazz.

Guitar Recorded Versions are transcribed by the best transcribers in the business. Every book contains notes and tablature. Visit **www.halleonard.com** for our complete selection.

00690169 Eric Johnson – Venus Isle $22.95
00122439 Jack Johnson – From Here to Now to You $22.99
00690846 Jack Johnson and Friends – Sing-A-Longs and Lullabies for the Film Curious George $19.95
00690271 Robert Johnson – The New Transcriptions $24.95
00699131 Best of Janis Joplin $19.95
00690427 Best of Judas Priest $22.99
00690277 Best of Kansas $19.95
00690911 Best of Phil Keaggy $24.99
00690727 Toby Keith Guitar Collection $19.99
00120814 Killswitch Engage – Disarm the Descent $22.99
00690504 Very Best of Albert King $19.95
00124869 Albert King with Stevie Ray Vaughan – In Session $22.99
00130447 B.B. King – Live at the Regal $17.99
00690444 B.B. King & Eric Clapton – Riding with the King $22.99
00690134 Freddie King Collection $19.95
00691062 Kings of Leon – Come Around Sundown $22.99
00690157 Kiss – Alive! $19.95
00690356 Kiss – Alive II $22.99
00694903 Best of Kiss for Guitar $24.95
00690355 Kiss – Destroyer $16.95
14026320 Mark Knopfler – Get Lucky $22.99
00690164 Mark Knopfler Guitar – Vol. 1 $19.95
00690163 Mark Knopfler/Chet Atkins – Neck and Neck $19.95
00690780 Korn – Greatest Hits, Volume 1 $22.95
00690377 Kris Kristofferson Collection $19.95
00690834 Lamb of God – Ashes of the Wake $19.95
00690875 Lamb of God – Sacrament $19.95
00690977 Ray LaMontagne – Gossip in the Grain $19.99
00690823 Ray LaMontagne – Trouble $19.95
00691057 Ray LaMontagne and the Pariah Dogs – God Willin' & The Creek Don't Rise $22.99
00690922 Linkin Park – Minutes to Midnight $19.95
00699623 The Best of Chuck Loeb $19.95
00114563 The Lumineers $22.99
00690525 Best of George Lynch $24.99
00690955 Lynyrd Skynyrd – All-Time Greatest Hits $22.99
00694954 New Best of Lynyrd Skynyrd $19.95
00690577 Yngwie Malmsteen – Anthology $24.95
00690754 Marilyn Manson – Lest We Forget $19.95
00694956 Bob Marley – Legend $19.95
00690548 Very Best of Bob Marley & The Wailers – One Love $22.99
00694945 Bob Marley – Songs of Freedom $24.95
00690914 Maroon 5 – It Won't Be Soon Before Long $19.95
00690657 Maroon 5 – Songs About Jane $19.95
00690748 Maroon 5 – 1.22.03 Acoustic $19.95
00690989 Mastodon – Crack the Skye $24.99
00119220 Brent Mason – Hot Wired $19.99
00691176 Mastodon – The Hunter $22.99
00137718 Mastodon – Once More 'Round the Sun $22.99
00690616 Matchbox Twenty – More Than You Think You Are $19.95
00691942 Andy McKee – Art of Motion $22.99
00691034 Andy McKee – Joyland $19.99
00120080 The Don McLean Songbook $19.95
00694952 Megadeth – Countdown to Extinction $22.95
00690244 Megadeth – Cryptic Writings $19.95
00694951 Megadeth – Rust in Peace $22.95
00690011 Megadeth – Youthanasia $22.99
00690505 John Mellencamp Guitar Collection $19.95
00690562 Pat Metheny – Bright Size Life $19.95
00691073 Pat Metheny with Christian McBride & Antonion Sanchez – Day Trip/Tokyo Day Trip Live $22.99
00690646 Pat Metheny – One Quiet Night $19.95
00690559 Pat Metheny – Question & Answer $19.95
00118836 Pat Metheny – Unity Band $22.99
00102590 Pat Metheny – What's It All About $22.99
00690040 Steve Miller Band Greatest Hits $19.95
00119338 Ministry Guitar Tab Collection $24.99
00102591 Wes Montgomery Guitar Anthology $24.99
00694802 Gary Moore – Still Got the Blues $22.99
00691005 Best of Motion City Soundtrack $19.99
00129884 Jason Mraz – Yes! $22.99
00690787 Mudvayne – L.D. 50 $22.95
00691070 Mumford & Sons – Sigh No More $22.99
00118196 Muse – The 2nd Law $19.99
00690996 My Morning Jacket Collection $19.99
00690984 Matt Nathanson – Some Mad Hope $22.99
00690611 Nirvana $22.95
00694895 Nirvana – Bleach $19.95
00694913 Nirvana – In Utero $19.95
00694883 Nirvana – Nevermind $19.95
00690026 Nirvana – Unplugged in New York $19.95
00120112 No Doubt – Tragic Kingdom $22.95
00690226 Oasis – The Other Side of Oasis $19.95
00307163 Oasis – Time Flies... 1994-2009 $19.99
00690818 The Best of Opeth $22.95
00691052 Roy Orbison – Black & White Night $22.99
00694847 Best of Ozzy Osbourne $22.95
00690399 Ozzy Osbourne – The Ozzman Cometh $22.99
00690933 Best of Brad Paisley $22.95
00690995 Brad Paisley – Play: The Guitar Album $24.99
00690939 Christopher Parkening – Solo Pieces $19.99
00690594 Best of Les Paul $19.95
00694855 Pearl Jam – Ten $22.99
00690439 A Perfect Circle – Mer De Noms $19.95
00690725 Best of Carl Perkins $19.99
00690499 Tom Petty – Definitive Guitar Collection $19.95
00690868 Tom Petty – Highway Companion $19.95
00690176 Phish – Billy Breathes $22.95
00691249 Phish – Junta $22.99
00121933 Pink Floyd – Acoustic Guitar Collection $22.99
00690428 Pink Floyd – Dark Side of the Moon $19.95
00690789 Best of Poison $19.95
00690299 Best of Elvis: The King of Rock 'n' Roll $19.95
00692535 Elvis Presley $19.95
00690925 The Very Best of Prince $22.99
00690003 Classic Queen $24.95
00694975 Queen – Greatest Hits $24.95
00690670 Very Best of Queensryche $19.95
00690878 The Raconteurs – Broken Boy Soldiers $19.95
00109303 Radiohead Guitar Anthology $24.99
00694910 Rage Against the Machine $19.95
00119834 Rage Against the Machine – Guitar Anthology $22.99
00690179 Rancid – And Out Come the Wolves $22.95
00690426 Best of Ratt $19.95
00690055 Red Hot Chili Peppers – Blood Sugar Sex Magik $19.95
00690584 Red Hot Chili Peppers – By the Way $19.95
00690379 Red Hot Chili Peppers – Californication $19.95
00690673 Red Hot Chili Peppers – Greatest Hits $19.95
00690090 Red Hot Chili Peppers – One Hot Minute $22.95
00691166 Red Hot Chili Peppers – I'm with You $22.99
00690852 Red Hot Chili Peppers – Stadium Arcadium $24.95
00690511 Django Reinhardt – The Definitive Collection $19.95
00690779 Relient K – MMHMM $19.95
00690643 Relient K – Two Lefts Don't Make a Right ... But Three Do $19.95
00690260 Jimmie Rodgers Guitar Collection $19.95
00138485 Kid Rock – Guitar Tab Collection $19.99
14041901 Rodrigo Y Gabriela and C.U.B.A. – Area 52 $24.99
00690014 Rolling Stones – Exile on Main Street $24.95
00690631 Rolling Stones – Guitar Anthology $27.95
00690685 David Lee Roth – Eat 'Em and Smile $19.95
00690031 Santana's Greatest Hits $19.95
00690796 Very Best of Michael Schenker $19.95
00128870 Matt Schofield Guitar Tab Collection $22.99
00690566 Best of Scorpions $22.95
00690604 Bob Seger – Guitar Anthology $22.99
00138870 Ed Sheeran – X $19.99
00690803 Best of Kenny Wayne Shepherd Band $19.95
00690750 Kenny Wayne Shepherd – The Place You're In $19.95
00690857 Shinedown – Us and Them $19.95
00122218 Skillet – Rise $22.99
00691114 Slash – Guitar Anthology $24.99
00690872 Slayer – Christ Illusion $19.95
00690813 Slayer – Guitar Collection $19.95
00690419 Slipknot $19.95
00690973 Slipknot – All Hope Is Gone $22.99
00690330 Social Distortion – Live at the Roxy $19.95
00120004 Best of Steely Dan $24.95
00694921 Best of Steppenwolf $22.95
00690655 Best of Mike Stern $19.95
14041588 Cat Stevens – Tea for the Tillerman $19.99
00690949 Rod Stewart Guitar Anthology $19.99
00690021 Sting – Fields of Gold $19.95
00690520 Styx Guitar Collection $19.95
00120081 Sublime $19.95
00690992 Sublime – Robbin' the Hood $19.99
00690519 SUM 41 – All Killer No Filler $19.95
00691072 Best of Supertramp $22.99
00690994 Taylor Swift $22.99
00690993 Taylor Swift – Fearless $22.99
00142151 Taylor Swift – 1989 $22.99
00115957 Taylor Swift – Red $21.99
00691063 Taylor Swift – Speak Now $22.99

RECORDED VERSIONS GUITAR®
AUTHENTIC TRANSCRIPTIONS WITH NOTES AND TABLATURE

00690767 Switchfoot – The Beautiful Letdown $19.95
00690531 System of a Down – Toxicity $19.95
00694824 Best of James Taylor $17.99
00694887 Best of Thin Lizzy $19.95
00690871 Three Days Grace – One-X $19.95
00690891 30 Seconds to Mars – A Beautiful Lie $19.95
00690233 The Merle Travis Collection $19.99
00690683 Robin Trower – Bridge of Sighs $19.95
00699191 U2 – Best of: 1980-1990 $19.95
00690732 U2 – Best of: 1990-2000 $19.95
00690894 U2 – 18 Singles $19.95
00124461 Keith Urban – Guitar Anthology $19.99
00690039 Steve Vai – Alien Love Secrets $24.95
00690172 Steve Vai – Fire Garden $24.95
00660137 Steve Vai – Passion & Warfare $24.95
00690881 Steve Vai – Real Illusions: Reflections $24.95
00694904 Steve Vai – Sex and Religion $24.95
00110385 Steve Vai – The Story of Light $22.99
00690392 Steve Vai – The Ultra Zone $19.95
00700555 Van Halen – Van Halen $19.99
00690024 Stevie Ray Vaughan – Couldn't Stand the Weather $19.95
00690370 Stevie Ray Vaughan and Double Trouble – The Real Deal: Greatest Hits Volume 2 $22.95
00690116 Stevie Ray Vaughan – Guitar Collection $24.95
00660136 Stevie Ray Vaughan – In Step $19.95
00694879 Stevie Ray Vaughan – In the Beginning $19.95
00660058 Stevie Ray Vaughan – Lightnin' Blues '83-'87 $24.95
00694835 Stevie Ray Vaughan – The Sky Is Crying $22.95
00690025 Stevie Ray Vaughan – Soul to Soul $19.95
00690015 Stevie Ray Vaughan – Texas Flood $19.95
00690772 Velvet Revolver – Contraband $22.95
00109770 Volbeat Guitar Collection $22.99
00121808 Volbeat – Outlaw Gentlemen & Shady Ladies $22.99
00690132 The T-Bone Walker Collection $19.95
00694789 Muddy Waters – Deep Blues $24.95
00690071 Weezer (The Blue Album) $19.95
00690516 Weezer (The Green Album) $19.95
00690286 Weezer – Pinkerton $19.95
00691046 Weezer – Rarities Edition $22.99
00117511 Whitesnake Guitar Collection $19.99
00690447 Best of the Who $24.95
00691941 The Who – Acoustic Guitar Collection $22.99
00691006 Wilco Guitar Collection $22.99
00690672 Best of Dar Williams $19.95
00691017 Wolfmother – Cosmic Egg $22.99
00690319 Stevie Wonder – Hits $19.99
00690596 Best of the Yardbirds $19.95
00690844 Yellowcard – Lights and Sounds $19.95
00690916 The Best of Dwight Yoakam $19.95
00691020 Neil Young – After the Goldrush $22.99
00691019 Neil Young – Everybody Knows This Is Nowhere $19.99
00690904 Neil Young – Harvest $29.99
00691021 Neil Young – Harvest Moon $22.99
00690905 Neil Young – Rust Never Sleeps $19.99
00690443 Frank Zappa – Hot Rats $19.95
00690624 Frank Zappa and the Mothers of Invention – One Size Fits All $22.99
00690623 Frank Zappa – Over-Nite Sensation $22.99
00121684 ZZ Top – Early Classics $24.99
00690589 ZZ Top – Guitar Anthology $24.95
00690960 ZZ Top Guitar Classics $19.99

HAL•LEONARD® CORPORATION
7777 W. Bluemound Rd. P.O. Box 13819 Milwaukee, WI 53213

Complete songlists and more at **www.halleonard.com**
Prices, contents, and availability subject to change without notice.

GUITAR *signature licks*

Signature Licks book/audio packs provide a step-by-step breakdown of "right from the record" riffs, licks, and solos so you can jam along with your favorite bands. They contain performance notes and an overview of each artist's or group's style, with note-for-note transcriptions in notes and tab. The CDs or online audio tracks feature full-band demos at both normal and slow speeds.

AC/DC
14041352......................$22.99

AEROSMITH 1973-1979
00695106......................$22.95

AEROSMITH 1979-1998
00695219......................$22.95

DUANE ALLMAN
00696042......................$22.99

BEST OF CHET ATKINS
00695752......................$22.95

AVENGED SEVENFOLD
00696473......................$22.99

BEST OF THE BEATLES FOR ACOUSTIC GUITAR
00695453......................$22.99

THE BEATLES BASS
00695283......................$22.95

THE BEATLES FAVORITES
00695096......................$24.95

THE BEATLES HITS
00695049......................$24.95

JEFF BECK
00696427......................$22.99

BEST OF GEORGE BENSON
00695418......................$22.95

BEST OF BLACK SABBATH
00695249......................$22.95

BLUES BREAKERS WITH JOHN MAYALL & ERIC CLAPTON
00696374......................$22.99

BLUES/ROCK GUITAR HEROES
00696381......................$19.99

BON JOVI
00696380......................$22.99

ROY BUCHANAN
00696654......................$22.99

KENNY BURRELL
00695830......................$22.99

BEST OF CHARLIE CHRISTIAN
00695584......................$22.95

BEST OF ERIC CLAPTON
00695038......................$24.95

ERIC CLAPTON – FROM THE ALBUM UNPLUGGED
00695250......................$24.95

BEST OF CREAM
00695251......................$22.95

CREEDANCE CLEARWATER REVIVAL
00695924......................$22.95

DEEP PURPLE – GREATEST HITS
00695625......................$22.95

THE BEST OF DEF LEPPARD
00696516......................$22.95

TOMMY EMMANUEL
00696409......................$22.99

ESSENTIAL JAZZ GUITAR
00695875......................$19.99

FAMOUS ROCK GUITAR SOLOS
00695590......................$19.95

FLEETWOOD MAC
00696416......................$22.99

BEST OF FOO FIGHTERS
00695481......................$24.95

ROBBEN FORD
00695903......................$22.95

BEST OF GRANT GREEN
00695747......................$22.99

BEST OF GUNS N' ROSES
00695183......................$24.99

THE BEST OF BUDDY GUY
00695186......................$22.99

JIM HALL
00695848......................$22.99

JIMI HENDRIX
00696560......................$24.99

JIMI HENDRIX – VOLUME 2
00695835......................$24.95

JOHN LEE HOOKER
00695894......................$19.99

BEST OF JAZZ GUITAR
00695586......................$24.95

ERIC JOHNSON
00699317......................$24.95

ROBERT JOHNSON
00695264......................$22.95

BARNEY KESSEL
00696009......................$22.99

THE ESSENTIAL ALBERT KING
00695713......................$22.95

B.B. KING – BLUES LEGEND
00696039......................$22.99

B.B. KING – THE DEFINITIVE COLLECTION
00695635......................$22.95

B.B. KING – MASTER BLUESMAN
00699923......................$24.99

MARK KNOPFLER
00695178......................$22.95

LYNYRD SKYNYRD
00695872......................$24.95

THE BEST OF YNGWIE MALMSTEEN
00695669......................$22.95

BEST OF PAT MARTINO
00695632......................$24.99

MEGADETH
00696421......................$22.99

WES MONTGOMERY
00695387......................$24.95

BEST OF NIRVANA
00695483......................$24.95

VERY BEST OF OZZY OSBOURNE
00695431......................$22.95

BRAD PAISLEY
00696379......................$22.99

BEST OF JOE PASS
00695730......................$22.95

JACO PASTORIUS
00695544......................$24.95

TOM PETTY
00696021......................$22.99

PINK FLOYD
00103659......................$24.99

PINK FLOYD – EARLY CLASSICS
00695566......................$22.95

BEST OF QUEEN
00695097......................$24.95

RADIOHEAD
00109304......................$24.99

BEST OF RAGE AGAINST THE MACHINE
00695480......................$24.95

RED HOT CHILI PEPPERS
00695173......................$22.95

RED HOT CHILI PEPPERS – GREATEST HITS
00695828......................$24.99

BEST OF DJANGO REINHARDT
00695660......................$24.95

BEST OF ROCK 'N' ROLL GUITAR
00695559......................$19.95

BEST OF ROCKABILLY GUITAR
00695785......................$19.95

BEST OF JOE SATRIANI
00695216......................$22.95

SLASH
00696576......................$22.99

THE BEST OF SOUL GUITAR
00695703......................$19.95

BEST OF SOUTHERN ROCK
00695560......................$19.95

STEELY DAN
00696015......................$22.99

MIKE STERN
00695800......................$24.99

BEST OF SURF GUITAR
00695822......................$19.95

STEVE VAI
00673247......................$22.95

STEVE VAI – ALIEN LOVE SECRETS: THE NAKED VAMPS
00695223......................$22.95

STEVE VAI – FIRE GARDEN: THE NAKED VAMPS
00695166......................$22.95

STEVE VAI – THE ULTRA ZONE: NAKED VAMPS
00695684......................$22.95

VAN HALEN
00110227......................$24.99

STEVIE RAY VAUGHAN – 2ND ED.
00699316......................$24.95

THE GUITAR STYLE OF STEVIE RAY VAUGHAN
00695155......................$24.95

BEST OF THE VENTURES
00695772......................$19.95

THE WHO – 2ND ED.
00695561......................$22.95

JOHNNY WINTER
00695951......................$22.99

YES
00113120......................$22.99

NEIL YOUNG – GREATEST HITS
00695988......................$22.99

BEST OF ZZ TOP
00695738......................$24.95

HAL•LEONARD®
CORPORATION
7777 W. BLUEMOUND RD. P.O. BOX 13819
MILWAUKEE, WISCONSIN 53213

www.halleonard.com

COMPLETE DESCRIPTIONS AND SONGLISTS ONLINE!
Prices, contents and availability subject to change without notice.

0516